JIM DAVIS

JIM DAVIS

by

JOHN MASEFIELD

Author of "Captain Margaret," "Martin Hyde," etc., etc.

GROSSET & DUNLAP

Publishers   NEW YORK

By arrangement with Frederick A. Stokes Company

Only Authorized American Edition

PRINTED IN THE UNITED STATES OF AMERICA

U. S. 736127

FOR JUDITH

CONTENTS

CHAPTER		PAGE
I	MY FIRST JOURNEY	1
II	NIGHT RIDERS	8
III	THE MAN ON THE MOUND	22
IV	THE HUT IN THE GORSE-BUSHES	39
V	THE LAST VOYAGE OF 'THE SNAIL'	58
VI	THE OWL'S CRY	72
VII	THE TWO COASTGUARDS	82
VIII	THE CAVE IN THE CLIFF	91
IX	SIGNING ON	104
X	ABOARD THE LUGGER	115
XI	THE FRIGATE 'LAOCOON'	124
XII	BLACK POOL BAY	134
XIII	IN THE VALLEY	147
XIV	A TRAITOR	160
XV	THE BATTLE ON THE SHORE	171
XVI	DRIFTING	186
XVII	THE 'BLUE BOAR'	198
XVIII	TRACKED	211
XIX	THE ROAD TO LONDON	221
XX	THE GIPSY CAMP	232

JIM DAVIS

JIM DAVIS

CHAPTER I

MY FIRST JOURNEY

I WAS born in the year 1800, in the town of Newnham-on-Severn, in Gloucestershire. I am sure of the year, because my father always told me that I was born at the end of the century, in the year that they began to build the great house. The house has been finished now these many years. The red-brick wall, which shuts its garden from the road (and the Severn), is all covered with valerian and creeping plants. One of my earliest memories is of the masons at work, shaping the two great bows. I remember how my nurse used to stop to watch them, at the corner of the road, on the green strip by the river-bank, where the gipsies camped on the way to Gloucester horse-fair. One of the masons was her sweetheart (Tom Farrell his name was), but he got into bad ways, I remember, and was hanged or transported, though that was years afterwards, when I had left that countryside.

My father and mother died when I was still a boy—my mother on the day of Trafalgar battle, in 1805, my father four years later. It was very sad at home after mother died; my father shut himself up in his study, never seeing anybody. When my father died, my uncle came to Newnham from his home in Devonshire; my old home was sold then, and I was taken away. I remember the day so very clearly. It was one sunny morning in early April. My uncle and I caught the coach at the top of the hill, at the door of the old inn opposite the church. The coachman had a hot drink handed up to him, and the ostlers hitched up the new team. Then the guard (he had a red coat, like a soldier) blew his horn, and the coach started off down the hill, going so very fast that I was afraid, for I had never ridden on a coach before, though I had seen them every day. The last that I saw of Newnham was the great house at the corner. It was finished by that time, of course, and as we drove past I saw the

MY FIRST JOURNEY 3

beautiful woman who lived there walking up and down the lawn with her husband, Captain Rylands, a very tall, handsome man, who used to give me apples. I was always afraid to eat the apples, because my nurse said that the Captain had killed a man. That was in the wars in Spain, fighting against the French.

I remember a great deal about my first coach-ride. We slept that night at Bristol in one of the famous coaching inns, where, as a great treat, I had bacon and eggs for supper, instead of bread-and-milk. In the morning, my uncle took me with him to the docks, where he had some business to do. That was the first time I ever really saw big ships, and that was the first time I spoke with the sailors. There was a capstan on one of the wharves, and men were at work, heaving round it, hoisting casks out of a West Indiaman. One of the men said, 'Come on, young master; give us a hand on the bar here.' So I put my hands on to the bar and pushed my best, walking beside him till my uncle called me away. There were many ships there at the time, all a West Indian convoy, and it was fine to see their great figure-heads, and the brass cannon at the ports, and to hear the men singing out aloft as they shifted spars and bent and unbent sails. They were all very lofty ships, built for speed; all were beautifully kept, like men-of-war, and all of them had their house-flags and red ensigns flying, so that in the sun they looked splendid. I shall never forget them.

After that, we went back to the inn, and climbed into another coach, and drove for a long, long time, often very slowly, till we reached a place near Newton Abbot, where there was a kind woman who put me to bed (I was too tired to notice more). Then, the next morning, I remember a strange man who was very cross at breakfast, so that the kind woman cried till my uncle sent me out of the room. It is funny how these things came back to me; it might have been only yesterday.

Late that afternoon we reached the south coast of Devon, so that we had the sea close beside us until the sun set. I heard the sea, as I thought, when we reached my uncle's house, at the end of the twilight; but they told me that it was a trout-stream, brawling over its boulders, and that the sea was a full mile away. My aunt helped to put me to

MY FIRST JOURNEY

bed, but I was too much excited to sleep well. I lay awake for a long, long time, listening to the noise of the brook, and to the wind among the trees outside, and to the cuckoo clock on the landing calling out the hours and half-hours. When I fell asleep I seemed to hear the sea and the crying out of the sailors. Voices seemed to be talking close beside me in the room; I seemed to hear all sorts of things, strange things, which afterwards really happened. There was a night-light burning on the wash-handstand. Whenever I woke up in the night the light would show me the shadow of the water jug upon the ceiling. It looked like an old, old man, with a humped back, walking the road, bowed over his cudgel.

I am not going to say very much about my life during the next few years. My aunt and uncle had no children of their own, and no great fondness for the children of others. Sometimes I was very lonely there; but after my tenth birthday I was at school most of my time, at Newton Abbot. I used to spend my Easter holidays (never more than a week) with the kind woman who put me to bed that night of my journey. My summer and winter holidays I spent with my uncle and aunt in their little house above the trout-stream.

The trout-stream rose about three miles from my uncle's house, in a boggy wood full of springs. It was a very rapid brook, nowhere more than three or four feet deep, and never more than twenty feet across, even near its mouth. Below my uncle's house it was full of little falls, with great mossy boulders which checked its flow, and pools where the bubbles spun. Further down, its course was gentler, for the last mile to the sea was a flat valley, with combes on each side covered with gorse and bramble. The sea had once come right up that valley to just below my uncle's house; but that was many years before—long before anybody could remember. Just after I went to live there, one of the farmers dug a drain, or 'rhine,' in the valley, to clear a boggy patch. He dug up the wreck of a large fishing-boat, with her anchor and a few rusty hoops lying beside her under the ooze about a foot below the surface. She must have sailed right up from the sea hundreds of years ago, before the brook's mouth got blocked with shingle (as I suppose it was) during some summer gale when the

MY FIRST JOURNEY

stream was nearly dry. Often, when I was a boy, I used to imagine the ships coming up from the sea, along that valley, firing their cannon. In the winter, when the snow melted, the valley would be flooded, till it looked just like a sea, and then I would imagine sea-fights there, with pirates in red caps boarding Spanish treasure galleons.

The sea-coast is mostly very bold in that part of Devon. Even where there are no cliffs, the land rises steeply from the sea, in grassy hills, with boulders and broken rock, instead of a beach, below them. There are small sandy beaches wherever the brooks run into the sea. Everywhere else the shore is 'steep-to'—so much so that in many places it is very difficult to reach the sea. I mention this because, later on, that steep coast gave me some queer adventures.

CHAPTER II

NIGHT-RIDERS

WHEN I was twelve years old, something very terrible happened, with good results for myself. The woman near Newton Abbot (I have spoken of her several times) was a Mrs Cottier, the wife of a school-master. Her husband used to drink very hard, and in this particular year he was turned out of the school, and lost his living. His wife left him then (or rather he left her; for a long time no one knew what became of him) and came to live with us, bringing with her little Hugh Cottier, her son, a boy of about my own age. After that, life in my uncle's house was a different thing to me. Mrs Cottier was very beautiful and kind; she was like my mother, strangely like, always sweet and gentle, always helpful and wise. I think she was the dearest woman who ever lived. I was always proud

NIGHT-RIDERS

when she asked me to do something for her.

Once, I remember (in the winter after Mrs Cottier came to us), she drove to Salcombe to do her Christmas shopping. It came on to snow during the afternoon; and at night-time the storm grew worse. We put back supper, expecting her to come in at any minute, but she did not come. The hours went by, and still she did not come, and still the storm worsened. The wind was not very high, but the air was full of a fine, powdery, drifting snow; the night seemed full of snow; snow fell down the chimney and drifted in under the door. My uncle was too lame with sciatica to leave his bed; and my aunt, always a woman of poor spirit, was afraid of the night. At eight o'clock I could stand it no longer, so I said that I would saddle the pony, and ride out along the Salcombe road to find her. Hugh was for going in my place; but Hugh was not so strongly built as I, and I felt that Hugh would faint after an hour in the cold. I put on double clothes, with an oilskin jacket over all, and then lit the lantern, and beat out of the house to the stable. I put one or two extra candles in my pockets, with a flint and steel, and some bread and meat. Something prompted me to take a hank of cord, and a heavy old boat-rug; and with all these things upon him old Greylegs, the pony, was heavy-laden.

When we got into the road together, I could not see a yard in front of me. There was nothing but darkness and drifting snow and the gleam of the drifts where the light of the lantern fell. There was no question of losing the road; for the road was a Devon lane, narrow and deep, built by the ancient Britons, so everybody says, to give them protection as they went down to the brooks for water. If it had been an open road, I could never have found my way for fifty yards. I was strongly built for a boy; even at sea I never suffered much from the cold, and this night was not intensely cold— snowy weather seldom is. What made the ride so exhausting was the beating of the snow into my eyes and mouth. It fell upon me in a continual dry feathery pelting, till I was confused and tired out with the effort of trying to see ahead. For a little while, I had the roar of the trout-stream in my ears to comfort me; but when I topped the next combe that died away; and there I was in the night, beating on against the storm, with the strange moaning sound of the wind from Dartmoor, and the snow rustling to keep me company. I was not exactly afraid, for the snow in my face bothered me too much, but often the night would seem full of people—laughing, horrible people —and often I would think that I saw Mrs Cottier lying half-buried in a drift.

I rode three miles or more without seeing anybody. Then, just before I reached the moor cross-roads, in a lull when the snow was not so bad, I heard a horse whinny, and old Greylegs baulked. Then I heard voices and a noise as of people riding; and before I could start old Greylegs I saw a party of horsemen crossing my road by the road from the sea to Dartmoor. They were riding at a quick trot, and though there were many horses (some thirty or forty), I could see, even in that light, that most of them were led. There were not more than a dozen men; and only one of all that dozen carried a lantern. Something told me that they were out for no good, and the same instinct made

me cover my lantern with my coat, so that
they passed me without seeing me. At first
I thought that they were the fairy troop, and
that gave me an awful fear; but a moment
later, in the wind, I felt a whiff of tobacco,
and of a strong, warm, sweet smell of spirits,
and I knew then that they were the night-
riders or smugglers. After they had gone, I
forced old Greylegs forward, and trotted on,
against the snow for another half-mile, with
my heart going thump upon my ribs. I
had an awful fear that they would turn,
and catch me; and I knew that the night-
riders wanted no witnesses of their adventures
in the dark.

About four miles from home, I came to
an open part of the road, where the snow
came down in its full fury, there being no
hedge to give a little shelter. It was so
thick that I could not get Greylegs to go
on. He stood stock-still, and cowered, though
I beat him with my hank of cord, and kicked
his ribs. It was cruel of me; but I thought
of Mrs Cottier, with her beautiful kind face,
lying in a drift of snow, and the thought was
dreadful to me. I got down from the saddle,
and put my lantern on the ground, and tried

NIGHT-RIDERS

to drag him forward, but it was useless. He would not have stirred if I had lighted a fire under him. When he had the instinct to stand still, nothing would make him budge a yard. A very fierce gust came upon me then. The snow seemed to whirl upon me from all sides, so that I got giddy and sick. And then, just at the moment, there were horses and voices all about me, coming from Salcombe way. Somebody called out, 'Hullo,' and somebody called out 'Look out, behind;' and then a lot of horses pulled up suddenly, and some men spoke, and a led horse shied at my lantern. I had no time to think or to run. I felt myself backing into old Greylegs in sheer fright; and then some one thrust a lantern into my face, and asked me who I was. By the light of the lantern I saw that he wore a woman's skirt over his trousers; and his face was covered by one of those great straw bee-skeps, pierced with holes for his eyes and mouth. He was one of the most terrible things I have ever seen.

'Why, it's a boy,' said the terrible man. 'What are you doing here, boy?'

Another man, who seemed to be a leader, called out from his horse, 'Who are you?'

but I was too scared to answer; my teeth were rattling in my head.

'It's a trick,' said another voice. 'We had best go for the moor.'

'Shut up,' said the leader, sharply. 'The boy's scared.'

He got down from his horse, and peered at me by the lantern light. He, too, wore a bee-skep; in fact, they all did, for there is no better disguise in the world, while nothing makes a man look more horrible. I was not quite so terrified by this time, because he had spoken kindly.

'Who are you?' he asked. 'We shan't eat you. What are you doing here?'

As well as I could I told him. The leader strode off a few paces, and spoke with one or two other men; but I could only catch the words, 'Yes; yes, Captain,' spoken in a low, quick voice, which seemed somehow familiar. Then he came back to me, and took me by the throat, and swayed me to and fro, very gently, but in a way which made me feel that I was going to be killed.

'Tell me,' he said, 'I shall know whether you're lying, so tell the truth, now. What have you seen to-night?'

NIGHT-RIDERS

I told him that I had seen a troop of horsemen going through the snow towards the moor.

'That settles it, Captain,' said another voice. 'You can't trust a young chap like that.'

'Shut up,' said the man they called Captain; 'I'm master, not you.'

He strode off again, to speak to another man. I heard some one laugh a little, and then the Captain came back to me. He took me by the throat as before, and again shook me. 'You listen to me,' he said, grimly. 'If you breathe so much as one word of what you've seen to-night—well—I shall know. D'ye hear? I shall know. And when I know—well—your little neck'll go. There's poetry. That will help you remember—

> 'When I know,
> Your neck'll go
> Like so.'

He gave a sharp little twist of his hand upon my Adam's apple.

I was terrified. I don't know what I said; my tongue seemed to wither on its stalk. The Captain walked to his horse, and remounted. 'Come along, boys,' he said. The

line of horses started off again. A hand fell
upon my shoulder, and a voice spoke kindly
to me. 'See here,' it said, 'you go on another
half-mile, you'll find a barn by the side of
the road. There's no door on the barn, and
you'll see a fire inside. You'll find your
lady there. She is safe all right. You keep
your tongue shut now.'

The speaker climbed into his saddle, and
trotted off into the night. 'Half a mile.
Straight ahead!' he called; then the dull
trampling died away, and I was left alone again
with Greylegs. Some minutes passed before
I could mount; for I was stiff with fright.
I was too frightened after that to mind the
snow; I was almost too frightened to ride.
Luckily for me the coming of the night-
riders had startled old Greylegs also; he
trotted on gallantly, though sometimes he
floundered into a drift, and had to be helped
out.

Before I came to the barn the snow stopped
falling, except for a few aimless flakes, which
drifted from all sides in the air. It was very
dark still; the sky was like ink; but there
was a feel of freshness (I cannot describe it)
which told me that the wind had changed.

NIGHT-RIDERS

Presently I saw the barn ahead of me, to the right of the road, spreading a red glow of fire across the way. Old Greylegs seemed glad of the sight; he gave a whinny and snorted. As well as he could he broke into a canter, and carried me up to the door in style.

'Are you safe, Mrs Cottier?' I called out.

'What! Jim!' she answered. 'How good of you to come for me!'

The barn, unlike most barns in that country, was of only one story. It may have been a farmhouse in the long ago, for it had larger windows than most barns. These had been stuffed with sacks and straw, to keep out the weather. The door had been torn from its place by some one in need of firewood; the roof was fairly sound; the floor was of trampled earth. Well away from the doorway, in the centre of the barn, some one had lighted a fire, using (as fuel) one of the faggots stacked against the wall. The smoke had long since blown out of doors. The air in the barn was clear and fresh. The fire had died down to a ruddy heap of embers, which glowed and grew grey again, as the draughts fanned them from the doorway. By the light of the fire I could see Mrs Cottier, sitting on the floor, with her back against the wheel of her trap, which had been dragged inside to be out of the snow. I hitched old Greylegs to one of the iron bolts, which had once held a door-hinge, and ran to her to make sure that she was unhurt.

'How in the world did you get here?' I asked. 'Are you sure you're not hurt?'

She laughed a little at this, and I got out my stores, and we made our supper by the fire. 'Where's old Nigger?' I asked her; for I was puzzled by seeing no horse.

'Oh, Jim,' she said, 'I've had such adventures.'

When she had eaten a little she told me her story.

'I was coming home from Salcombe,' she said, 'and I was driving fast, so as to get home before the snow lay deep. Just outside Southpool, Nigger cast a shoe, and I was kept waiting at the forge for nearly half an hour. After that, the snow was so bad that I could not get along. It grew dark when I was only a mile or two from the blacksmith's, and I began to fear that I should never get home. However, as I drove through Stokenham, the weather seemed to

NIGHT-RIDERS

clear a little, so I hurried Nigger all I could, hoping to get home in the lull. When I got to within a hundred yards from here, in the little hollow, where the stunted ashes are, I found myself among a troop of horsemen, who stopped me, and asked me a lot of questions. They were all disguised, and they had lanterns among them, and I could see that the horses carried tubs; I suppose full of smuggled lace and brandy and tobacco, ready to be carried inland. Jim, dear, I was horribly frightened; for while they were speaking together I thought I heard the voice of—of some one I know—or used to know.'

She stopped for a moment overcome, and I knew at once that she was speaking of her husband, the schoolmaster that was. 'And then,' she continued, 'some of them told me to get down out of the trap. And then another of them seized Nigger's head, and walked the trap as far as the barn here. Then they unharnessed Nigger, and led him away, saying they were short of horses, but would send him back in a day or two. They seemed to know all about me, where I lived, and everything. One of them took a faggot from a wall here, and laid the big fire.

with straw instead of paper. While he lit it he kept his great bee-skep on his head (they all wore them), but I noticed he had three blue rings tattooed on his left ring-finger. Now, somewhere I have seen a man, quite recently, with rings tattooed like that, only I can't remember where. I wish I could think where. He was very civil and gentle. He saw that the fire burnt up well, and left me all those sticks and logs, as well as the flint and steel, in case it should go out before the snow stopped. Oh, and he took the rugs out of the trap, and laid them on the ground for me to sit on. Before he left, he said, very civilly, 'I am sure you don't want to get folks into trouble, madam. Perhaps you won't mention this, in case they ask you.' So I said that I didn't want to get people into trouble; but that it was hardly a manly act to leave a woman alone, in an open barn, miles from anywhere, on a night like to-night. He seemed ashamed at this; for he slunk off, saying something about "only obeying orders," and "not having much choice in the matter." Then they all stood about outside, in the snow, leaving me alone here. They must have stayed outside a couple of hours.

About a quarter of an hour before you came I heard some one call out, 'There it is, boys!' and immediately they all trotted off, at a smart pace. They must have seen or heard some signal. Of course, up here on the top of the combe, one could see a long way if the snow lulled for a moment.'

CHAPTER III

THE MAN ON THE MOUND

It was very awesome sitting there by the firelight in the lonely barn, hearing the strange moan of the snow-wind. When Mrs Cottier finished her story we talked of all sorts of things; I think that we were both a little afraid of being silent in such a place, so, as we ate, we kept talking just as though we were by the fireside at home. I was afraid that perhaps the revenue officers would catch us there and force us to tell all we knew, and I was dreadfully frightened when I remembered the captain in the bee-skep who had shaken my throat and given me such a warning to be silent. When we had finished our supper, I told Mrs Cottier that perhaps we could harness old Greylegs to the trap, but this she thought would never do, as the drifts on the road made it such bad going; at last I persuaded her to mount

THE MAN ON THE MOUND

old Greylegs and to ride astride like a boy, or like so many of the countrywomen in our parts. When she had mounted I took the old pony by the head and led him out, carrying the lantern in my hand.

When we got outside we found, to our great surprise, that the sky had cleared—it was a night of stars now that the wind had changed. By the 'blink' of the snow our road was quite plain to us, and the sharp touch of frost in the air (which we felt all the more after our bonfire in the barn) had already made the snow crisp underfoot. It was pleasant to be travelling like that so late at night with Mrs Cottier; I felt like a knight who had just rescued a princess from a dragon; we talked together as we had never talked before. Whenever we climbed a bad combe she dismounted, and we walked together hand in hand like dear friends. Once or twice in the quiet I thought I heard the noise of the excisemen's horses, and then my heart thumped in my throat; then, when I knew myself mistaken, I felt only the delight of being of service to this dear woman who walked by me so merrily.

When we came to the foot of the combe,

to the bridge over the trout-stream, she stopped for a moment. 'Jim,' she said, drawing me to her, 'I shall never forget to-night, nor the little friend who rode out to help me; I want you, after this, always to look on me as your mother—I knew your mother a little, years ago. Well, dear, try to think of me as you would of her, and be a brother to my Hugh, Jim: let us all three be one family.' She stooped down and kissed my cheek and lips.

'I will, Mrs Cottier,' I said; 'I'll always be a brother to Hugh.' I was too deeply moved to say much more, for I had so long yearned for some woman like my mother to whom I could go for sympathy and to whom I could tell everything without the fear of being snubbed or laughed at. I just said, 'Thank you, Mims.' I don't know why I called her 'Mims' then, but I did, and afterwards I never called her anything else; that was my secret name for her. She kissed me again and stroked my cheek with her hand, and we went on again together up the last steep bit of road to the house. Always, after that, I never thought of Mrs Cottier without feeling her lips upon my cheek and hearing the stamp of old Greylegs as he pawed on the snow, eager for the stable just round the corner.

It was very nice to get round the corner and to see the lights of the house a little way in front of us; in a minute or two we were there. Mrs Cottier had been dragged in to the fire to all sorts of comforting drinks and exclamations, and old Greylegs was snug in his stable having his coat rubbed down before going to sleep under his rug. We were all glad to get to bed that night: Hugh and my aunt were tired with anxiety, and Mrs Cottier and I had had enough adventure to make us very thankful for rest.

Before we parted for the night she drew me to one side and told me that she had not mentioned the night-riders to my uncle and aunt while I was busy in the stable, and that it might be safer if I, too, kept quiet about them. I do not know how she explained the absence of Nigger, but I am sure they were all too thankful to have her safely home again to bother much about the details of her drive.

Hugh and I always slept in soldier's cot-beds in a little room looking out over the lane. During the night we heard voices, and footsteps moving in the lane beneath us, and our dog (always kennelled at the back of the house) barked a good deal. Hugh and I crept from our bed and peered through the window, but it opened the wrong way; we could only look down the lane, whereas the noise seemed to come from just above us, near the stable door; unluckily, the frost had covered the window with ice-flowers, so that we could not see through the glass. We were, however, quite certain that there were people with lights close to our stable door; we thought at first that we had better call Mrs Cottier, and then it flashed through my mind that these were the night-riders, come to return Nigger, so I told Hugh to go back to bed and forget about it. I waited at the window for a few moments, wondering if the men would pass the house; I felt a horrible longing to see those huge and ghastly things in skirts and bee-skeps striding across the snow, going home from their night's prowl like skulking foxes; but whoever they were they took no risks. Some one softly whistled a scrap of a tune ('Tom, Tom, the piper's son') as though he were pleased

THE MAN ON THE MOUND 27

at having finished a good piece of work, and then I heard footsteps going over the gap in the hedge and the crackling of twigs in the little wood on the other side of the lane. I went back to bed and slept like a top until nearly breakfast time.

I went out to the stable as soon as I was dressed, to find Joe Barnicoat, our man, busy at his morning's work; he had already swept away the snow from the doors of the house and stable, so that I could not see what footmarks had been made there since I went to fetch Greylegs at eight the night before. Joe was in a great state of excitement, for during the night the stable had been broken open. I had left it locked up, as it always was locked, after I had made Greylegs comfortable. When Joe came there at about half-past seven, he had found the broken padlock lying in the snow and the door-staple secured by a wooden peg cut from an ash in the hedge. As I expected, Nigger was in his stall, but the poor horse was dead lame from a cut in the fetlock: Joe said he must have been kicked there. I was surprised to find that the trap also had come home—there it was in its place with the snow still unmelted on its wheels. I helped Joe to dress poor Nigger's leg, saying that it was a pity we had not noticed it before. Joe was grumbling about 'some people not having enough sense to know when a horse was lame,' so I let him grumble.

When we had dressed the wound, I turned to the trap to lift out Mrs Cottier's parcels, which I carried indoors. Breakfast was ready on the table, and Mrs Cottier and Hugh were toasting some bread at the fire. My aunt was, of course, breakfasting upstairs with my uncle; he was hardly able to stir with sciatica, poor man; he needed somebody to feed him.

'Good morning, Mims dear,' I cried. 'What do you think? The trap's come back and here are all your parcels.' I noticed then (I had not noticed it before) that one of the parcels was very curiously wrapped. It was wrapped in an old sack, probably one of those which filled the windows of the barn, for bits of straw still stuck in the threads.

'Whatever have you got there, Jim?' said Mrs Cottier.

'One of your parcels,' I answered; 'I've just taken it out of the trap.'

'Let me see it,' she said. 'There must be some mistake. That's not one of mine.' She took the parcel from me and turned it over before opening it.

On turning the package over, we saw that some one had twisted a piece of dirty grey paper (evidently wrapping-paper from the grocer's shop) about the rope yarn which kept the roll secure. Mrs Cottier noticed it first. 'Oh,' she cried, 'there's a letter, too. I wonder if it's meant for me?'

We untied the rope yarn and the paper fell upon the table; we opened it out, wondering what message could be written on it. It was a part of a grocer's sugar bag, written upon in the coarse black crayon used by the tally-men on the quays at Kingsbridge. The writing was disguised, so as to give no clue to the writer; the letters were badly-formed printer's capitals; the words were ill-spelled, and the whole had probably been written in a hurry, perhaps by the light of our fire in the barn.

'Hors is laimd,' said the curious letter. 'Regret inconvenuns axept Respect from obt servt Captin Sharp.'

'Very sweet and to the point,' said Mrs Cottier. 'Is Nigger lame, then?'

'Yes,' I answered. 'Joe says he has been kicked. You won't be able to drive him for some time.'

'Poor old Nigger,' said Mrs Cottier, as she unwrapped the parcel. 'Now, I wonder what "Respec" Captain Sharp has sent me?'

She unrolled the sacking, and out fell two of those straw cases which are used to protect wine-bottles. They seemed unusually bulky, so we tore them open. In one of them there was a roll, covered with a bit of tarpaulin. It contained a dozen yards of very beautiful Malines lace. The other case was full of silk neckerchiefs packed very tightly, eleven altogether; most of them of uncoloured silk, but one of green and another of blue—worth a lot of money in those days, and perhaps worth more to-day, now that such fine silk is no longer woven.

'So this is what we get for the loan of Nigger, Jim,' said Mrs Cottier. 'We ought, by rights, to give these things to the revenue officer.'

'Yes,' I said, 'but if we do that, we shall have to say how they came, and why they

THE MAN ON THE MOUND 31

came, and then perhaps the exciseman will get a clue, and we shall have brought the night-riders into trouble.'

It was cowardly of me to speak like this; but you must remember that I had been in 'Captain Sharp's' hands the night before, and I was still terrified by his threat—

> 'When I know,
> Your neck'll go
> Like so.'

'Well,' said Mrs Cottier, looking at me rather sharply, 'we will keep the things, and say nothing about them: but we must find out what duty should be paid on them, and send it to the exciseman at Dartmouth. That will spare our consciences.'

After breakfast, Mrs Cottier went to give orders to the servant, while Hugh and I slipped down the lane to see how the snow had drifted in our little orchard by the brook. We had read somewhere that the Red Indians often make themselves snow-houses, or snow-burrows, when the winter is severe. We were anxious to try our hands at making a snow-house. We wanted to know whether a house with snow walls could really be warm, and we pictured to ourselves how strange it would be to be shut in by walls of snow, with only one little hole for air, seeing nothing but the white all round us, having no window to look through. We thought that it would be wonderful to have a snow-house, especially if snow fell after the roof had been covered in, for then no one could know if the dweller were at home. One would lie very still, wrapped up in buffalo robes, while all the time the other Indians would be prowling about in their war-paint, looking for you. Or perhaps the Spaniards would be after you with their bloodhounds, and you would get down under the snow in the forest somewhere, and the snow would fall and fall, covering your tracks, till nothing could be seen but a little tiny hole, melted by your breath, through which you got fresh air. Then you would hear the horses and the armour and the baying of the hounds; but they would never find you, though their horses' hoofs might almost sink through the snow to your body.

We went down to the orchard, Hugh and I, determined to build a snow-house if the drifts were deep enough. We were not going to plunge into a drift, and make a sort of chamber by wrestling our bodies about, as the Indians do. We had planned to dig a square chamber in the biggest drift we could find, and then to roof it over with an old tarpaulin stretched upon sticks. We were going to cover the tarpaulin with snow, in the Indian fashion, and we had planned to make a little narrow passage, like a fox's earth, as the only doorway to the chamber.

It was a bright, frosty morning: the sun shone, the world sparkled, the sky was of a dazzling blue, the snow gleamed everywhere. Hoolie, the dog, was wild with excitement. He ran from drift to drift, snapping up mouthfuls of snow, and burrowing down sideways till he was half buried.

There was a flower garden at one end of the orchard, and in the middle of the garden there was a summer-house. The house was a large, airy single room (overlooking the stream), with a space beneath it, half-cave, half-cellar, open to the light, where Joe Barnicoat kept his gardening tools, with other odds-and-ends, such as bast, peasticks, sieves, shears, and traps for birds and vermin. Hugh and I went directly to this lower chamber to get a shovel for our work. We stood at the entrance for a moment to watch Hoolie playing in the snow; and as we watched, something caught my eye and made me look up sharply.

Up above us, on the side of the combe beyond the lane, among a waste of gorse, in full view of the house (and of the orchard where we were), there was a mound or barrow, the burial-place of an ancient British king. It was a beautifully-rounded hill, some twenty-five feet high. A year or two before I went there it had been opened by the vicar, who found inside it a narrow stone passage, leading to an inner chamber, walled with unmortared stone. In the central chamber there were broken pots, a few bronze spear-heads, very green and brittle, and a mass of burnt bones. The doctor said that they were the bones of horses. On the top of all this litter, with his head between his knees, there sat a huge skeleton. The vicar said that when alive the man must have been fully six feet six inches tall, and large in proportion, for the bones were thick and heavy. He had evidently been a king: he wore a soft gold circlet round his head, and three golden bangles on his arms. He had been killed

THE MAN ON THE MOUND 35

in battle. In the side of his skull just above the circle of gold, there was a great wound, with a flint axe-blade firmly wedged in the bone. The vicar had often told me about this skeleton. I remember to this day the shock of horror which came upon me when I heard of this great dead king, sitting in the dark among his broken goods, staring out over the valley. The country people always said that the hill was a fairy hill. They believed that the pixies went to dance there whenever the moon was full. I never saw the pixies myself, but somehow I always felt that the hill was uncanny. I never passed it at night if I could avoid it.

Now, when I looked up, as I stood with Hugh watching the dog, I saw something flash upon the top of the barrow. In that bright sun, with all the snow about, many things were sparkling; but this thing gleamed like lightning, suddenly, and then flashed again. Looking at it sharply, I saw that there was a man upon the barrow top, apparently lying down upon the snow. He had something in his hand turned to the sun, a piece of glass perhaps, or a tin plate, some very bright thing, which flashed. He flashed it three times quickly, then paused, then flashed it again. He seemed to be looking intently across the valley to the top of the combe beyond, to the very place where the road from Salcombe swings round to the dip. Looking in that direction, I saw the figure of a man standing on the top of the wall against a stunted holly-tree at the curve of the road. I had to look intently to see him at all, for he was in dark clothes, which shaded off unnoticed against the leaves of the holly. I saw him jump down now and again, and disappear round the curve of the road as though to look for something. Then he would run back and flash some bright thing once, as though in answer to the man on the barrow.

It seemed to me very curious. I nudged Hugh's arm, and slipped into the shelter of the cave. For a few moments we watched the signaller. Then, suddenly, the watcher at the road-bend came running back from his little tour up the road, waving his arms, and flashing his bright plate as he ran. We saw him spring to his old place on the wall, and jump from his perch into the ditch. He had some shelter there, for we could see his head

THE MAN ON THE MOUND 37

peeping out above the snow like an apple among straw. We were so busy watching the head among the snow that we did not notice the man upon the barrow. Something made us glance towards him, and, to our surprise and terror, we saw him running across the orchard more than half-way towards us. In spite of the snow he ran swiftly. We were frightened, for he was evidently coming towards us. He saw that we saw him, and lifted one arm and swung it downwards violently, as though to bid us lie down.

I glanced at Hugh and he at me, and that was enough. We turned at once, horribly scared, and ran as fast as we could along the narrow garden path, then over the wall, stumbling in our fright, into the wood. We did not know why we ran nor where we were going. We only felt that this strange man was after us, coming in great bounds to catch us. We were too frightened to run well; even had there been no snow upon the ground we could not have run our best. We were like rabbits pursued by a stoat, we seemed to have lost all power in our legs.

We had a good start. Perhaps without

that fear upon us we might have reached the house, but as it was we felt as one feels in a nightmare, unable to run though in an agony of terror. Getting over the wall was the worst, for there Hugh stumbled badly, and I had to turn and help him, watching the man bounding ever nearer, signing to us to stay for him. A minute later, as we slipped and stumbled through the scrub of the wood, we heard him close behind us, crying to us in a smothered voice to stop. We ran on, terrified; and then Hugh's foot caught in a briar, so that he fell headlong with a little cry.

I turned at once to help him up, feeling like the doe rabbit, which turns (they say) against a weasel, to defend its young ones. It sounds brave of me, but it was not: I was scared almost out of my wits.

CHAPTER IV

THE HUT IN THE GORSE-BUSHES

THE man was on us in three strides, with his hand on our collars, frightening us out of any power to struggle. 'You young fools,' he said, not unkindly. 'Why couldn't you stop when I waved to you?'

We did not answer, nor did he seem to expect us to answer. He just swung us round with our faces from the house, and hurried us, at a smart run, down the road. 'Don't you stir a muscle,' he added as he ran. 'I'm not going to eat you, unless you drive me to it.'

At the lower end of the wood, nearly half a mile from our home, the scrub was very thick. It seemed to be a tangle of briars, too thick for hounds—too thick, almost, for rabbits. Hugh and I had never been in that part of the wood before, but our guide evidently knew it well, for he never hesitated.

He swung us on, panting as we were, along the clearer parts, till we came to a part where our way seemed stopped by gorse-bushes. They rose up, thick and dark, right in front of us. Our guide stopped and told us to look down. Among the gnarled gorse-stems there seemed to be a passage or 'run' made by some beast, fox or badger, going to and from his lair.

'Down you go,' said our guide. 'There's lots of room when you try. Imagine you're a rabbit.'

We saw that it was useless to say No; and, besides, by this time we had lost most of our terror. I dropped on to my knees at once, and began to squirm through the passage. Hugh followed me, and the strange man followed after Hugh. It was not really difficult, except just at the beginning, where the stems were close together. When I had wriggled for a couple of yards, the bushes seemed to open out to either side. It was prickly work, but I am sure that we both felt the romance of it, forgetting our fear before we reached the heart of the clump.

In the heart of the clump the gorse-bushes had been cut away, and piled up in a sort of

HUT IN THE GORSE-BUSHES 41

wall about a small central square some five or six yards across. In the middle of the square some one had dug a shallow hollow, filling rather more than half of the open space. The hollow was about eighteen inches deep, and roughly paved with shingle from the beach, well stamped down into the clay. It had then been neatly wattled over into a sort of trim hut, like the huts the salmon-fishers used to build near Kingsbridge. The wattling was made fairly waterproof by masses of gorse and bracken driven in among the boughs. It was one of the most perfect hiding-places you could imagine. It could not be seen from any point, save from high up in one of the trees surrounding the thicket. A regiment might have beaten the wood pretty thoroughly, and yet have failed to find it. The gorse was so thick in all the outer part of the clump that dogs would leave its depths unsearched. Yet, lying there in the shelter one could hear the splashing babble of the brook only fifty yards away, and the singing of a girl at the mill a little further up the stream.

The man told us to get inside the shelter, which we did. Inside it was rather dark, but the man lit a lantern which hung from the roof and kindled a fire in a little fireplace. This fireplace was covered with turf, so that the smoke should not rise up in a column. We saw that the floor of the hut was heaped with bracken, and there were tarpaulin boat-rugs piled in one corner, as though for bedding.

The man picked up a couple of rugs and told us to wrap ourselves in them. 'You'll be cold if you don't wrap up,' he said.

As he tucked the rugs about us I noticed that the ring finger of his left hand was tattooed with three blue rings. I remembered what Mrs Cottier had said about the man who had lighted her fire in the barn, so I stared at him hard, trying to fix his features on my memory. He was a well-made, active-looking man, with great arms and shoulders. He was evidently a sailor: one could tell that by the way of his walk, by the way in which his arms swung, by the way in which his head was set upon his body. What made him remarkable was the peculiar dancing brightness of his eyes; they gave his face, at odd moments, the look of a fiend; then that look would go, and he would look like a mischievous, merry boy; but more generally he would look fierce and resolute. Then his straight mouth would set, his eyes puckered in as though he were looking out to windward, the scar upon his cheek twitched and turned red, and he looked most wrathful and terrible.

'Well, mister,' the man said to me, 'would you know me again, in case you saw me?'

'Yes,' I said, 'I should know you anywhere.'

'Would you,' he said grinning. 'Well, I was always the beauty of the bunch.' He bit off a piece of plug tobacco and began to chew it. By-and-by he turned to Hugh to ask if he chewed tobacco. Hugh answered 'No,' laughing.

'Ah,' said the man, 'don't you learn. That's my advice. It's not easy to stop, once you begin.'

He lay back in his corner, and seemed to pass into a sort of day-dream. Presently he looked up at us again, and asked us if we knew why we were there. We said that we did not.

'Well,' he said, 'it's like this. Last night you' (here he gave me a nudge with his foot) 'you young gentleman that looks so smart, you went for a ride late at night, in the snow and all. See what came of it. There was others out for a ride last night, quite a lot of 'em. Others that the law would be glad to know of, with men so scarce for the King's navy. Well, to-day the beaks are out trying to find them other ones. There's a power of red-coats come here, besides the preventives, and there they go, clackity clank, all swords and horses, asking at every house.'

'What do they ask,' said Hugh.

'They ask a lot of things,' said the man. '"Where was you last night?" That's one question. "What time did you come in last night?" That's another. "Let's have a look at your horse; he looks as though he'd bin out in the snow last night." Lots of things they ask, and if they got a hold of you, young master, why, you might have noticed things last night, and perhaps they might pump what you noticed out of you. So some one thinks you had best be out of the road when they come.'

'Who is someone?' I asked.

'Just some one,' he answered. 'Some one who gets more money than I get.' His mouth drew into a hard and cruel line; he

HUT IN THE GORSE-BUSHES 45

lapsed into his day-dream, still chewing his plug of tobacco. 'Some one,' he added, 'who don't like questions, and don't like to be talked about too much.'

He was silent for a minute or two, while Hugh and I looked at each other.

'Oh, I'm not going to keep you long,' said the man. 'Them redcoats'll have done asking questions about here before your dinner time. Then they'll ride on, and a good riddance. Your lady will know how to answer them all right. But till they're gone, why, here you'll stay. So let's be comp'ny. What's your name, young master?' He gave Hugh a dig in the ribs with his boot.

'Hugh,' he answered.

'Hugh,' said the man: 'Hugh! You won't never come to much, you won't. What's *your* name?' He nudged me in the same way.

'Jim,' I said.

'Ah! Jim, Jim,' he repeated. 'I've known a many Jims. Some were good in their way, too.' He seemed to shrink into himself suddenly—I can't explain it—but he seemed to shrink, like a cat crouched to spring, and his eyes burned and danced; they seemed to look right into me, horribly gleaming, till the whole man became, as it were, just two bright spots of eyes—one saw nothing else.

'Ah,' he said, after a long, cruel glare at me, 'this is the first time Jim and I ever met. The first time. We shall be great friends, we shall. We shall be better acquainted, you and I. I wouldn't wonder if I didn't make a man of you, one time or another. Give me your hand, Jim.'

I gave him my hand; he looked at it under the lantern; he traced one or two of the lines with his blackened finger-nails, muttering some words in a strange language, which somehow made my flesh creep. He repeated the words: 'Orel. Orel. Adartha Cay.' Then he glanced at the other hand, still muttering, and made a sort of mark with his fingers on my forehead. Hugh told me afterwards that he seemed to trace a kind of zigzag on my left temple. All the time he was muttering he seemed to be half-conscious, almost in a trance, or as if he were mad: he frightened us dreadfully. After he had made the mark upon my brow he came to himself again.

'They will see it,' he muttered. 'It'll

HUT IN THE GORSE-BUSHES 47

be bright enough. The mark. It'll shine. They'll know when they see it. It is very good. A very good sign: it burns in the dark. They'll know it over there in the night.' Then he went on mumbling to himself, but so brokenly that we could catch only a few words here and there—'black and red, knowledge and beauty; red and black, pleasure and strength. What do the cards say?'

He opened his thick sea-coat, and took out a little packet of cards from an oil-skin case. He dealt them out, first of all, in a circle containing two smaller circles; then in a curious sort of five-pointed star; lastly, in a square with a circle cutting off the corners. 'Queer, queer,' he said, grinning, as he swept the cards up and returned them to his pocket. 'You and I will know a power of queer times together, Jim.'

He brightened up after that, as though something had pleased him very much. He looked very nice when he looked pleased, in spite of his eyes and in spite of the gipsy darkness of his skin. 'Here,' he said, 'let's be company. D'ye know any knots, you two?'

No; neither of us knew any knots except the ordinary overhand and granny knots.

'Well, I'll show you,' he said. 'It'll come in useful some day. Always learn what you can, that's what I say, because it'll come in useful. That's what the Irishman said. Always learn what you can. You never know; that's the beauty of it.'

He searched in his pockets till he found a small hank of spunyarn, from which he cut a piece about a yard long. 'See here,' he said. 'Now, I'll teach you. It's quite easy, if you only pay attention. Now, how would you tie a knot if you was doing up a parcel?'

We both tried, and both made granny knots, with the ends sticking out at right angles to the rest of the yarn.

'Wrong,' he said. 'Those are grannies. They would jam so that you'll never untie 'em, besides being ugly. There's wrong ways even in doing up a string. See here.' He rapidly twisted the ends together into a reef-knot. 'There's strength and beauty together,' he said. 'Look how neat it is, the ends tidy along the standing part all so neat as pie. Besides, it'd never jam. Watch how I do it, and then try it for yourself.'

HUT IN THE GORSE-BUSHES

Very soon we had both mastered the reef-knot, and had tried our hand at others—the bow-line, the figure of eight, the Carrick bend, and the old swab-hitch. He was very patient with us. He told us exactly how each knot would be used at sea, and when, and why, and what the officers would say, and how things would look on deck while they were in the doing. The time passed pleasantly and quickly; we felt like jolly robbers in a cave. It was like being the hero of a story-book to sit there with that rough man waiting till the troops had gone. It was not very cold with the fire and the boat-rugs. We were heartily sorry when the man rose to his feet, with the remark that he must see if the coast were clear. Before he left the hut he glared down at us. 'Look here,' he said, 'don't you try to go till I give the word. But there, we're friends; no need to speak rough to friends. I'll be back in a minute.'

The strange man passed out of the hut and along the rabbit-run to the edge of the gorse. We heard his feet crunch upon the snow beyond, rustling the leaves underneath it; and then it was very, very quiet again, though once, in the stillness, we heard a cock pheasant calling. Another pheasant answered him from somewhere above at the upper part of the wood, and it occurred to both of us that the pheasants were the night-riders, making their private signals.

'We've had a famous adventure to tell Mother,' said Hugh.

'Yes,' I said; 'but we had better be careful not to tell anybody else. I wonder what they do here in this hut; I suppose they hide their things here till it's safe to take them away.'

'Where do they take them?' asked Hugh.

'Away into Dartmoor,' I said. 'And there there are wonderful places, so old Evans the postboy told me.'

'What sort of places?' asked Hugh.

'Oh caves covered over with gorse and fern, and old copper and tin mines, which were worked by the ancient Britons. They go under the ground for miles, so old Evans told me, with passages, and steps up and down, and great big rooms cut in the rock. And then there are bogs where you can sink things till it's quite safe to take them up. The bog-water keeps them quite sound; it

HUT IN THE GORSE-BUSHES 51

doesn't rot them like ordinary water. Sometimes men fall into the bogs, and the marsh-mud closes over them. That's the sort of place Dartmoor is.'

Hugh was very much interested in all this, but he was a quiet boy, not fond of talking. 'Yes,' he said; 'but where do the things go afterwards—who takes them?'

'Nobody knows, so old Evans said,' I answered; 'but they go, they get taken. People come at night and carry them to the towns, little by little, and from the market towns, they get to the cities, no one knows how. I daresay this hut has been full of things—valuable lace and silk, and all sorts of wines and spirits—waiting for some one to carry them into the moor.'

'Hush!' said Hugh; 'there's some one calling—it's Mother.'

Outside the gorse-clump, at some little distance from us, we heard Mrs Cottier and my aunt calling 'Hugh!' and 'Jim!' repeatedly. We lay very still wondering what they would think, and hoping that they would make no search for us. They could have tracked us in the snow quite easily, but we knew very well they would never think of it, for they were both short-sighted and ignorant of what the Red Indians do when they go tracking. To our surprise their voices came nearer and nearer, till they were at the edge of the clump, but on the side opposite to that in which the rabbit-run opened. I whispered to Hugh to be quiet as they stopped to call us. They lingered for several minutes, calling every now and then, and talking to each other in between whiles. We could hear every word of their conversation.

'It's very curious,' said my aunt. 'Wherever can they have got to? How provoking boys are.'

'It doesn't really matter,' said Mims; 'the officer has gone, and the boy would only have been scared by all his questions. He might have frightened the boy out of his wits. I wonder where the young monkeys have got to. They were going to build snow-huts, like the Indians. Perhaps they're hiding in one now.'

We were, had she only known it; Hugh and I grinned at each other. Suddenly my aunt spoke again with a curious inflection in her voice.

HUT IN THE GORSE-BUSHES 53

'How funny,' she exclaimed.

'What is it?' asked Mrs Cottier.

'I'm almost sure I smell something burning,' said my aunt. 'I'm sure I do. Don't you?'

There was a pause of a few seconds while the two ladies sniffed the air.

'Yes,' said Mrs Cottier, 'there is something burning. It seems to come from that gorse there.'

'Funny,' said my aunt. 'I suppose some one has lighted a fire up in the wood and the smoke is blowing down on us. Well, we'll go in to dinner; it's no good staying here catching our death looking for two mad things. I suppose you didn't hear how Mrs Burns is, yesterday?'

The two ladies passed away from the clump towards the orchard, talking of the affairs of the neighbourhood. A few minutes after they had gone, a cock pheasant called softly a few yards from us, then the gorse-stems shook, and our friend appeared at the hut door.

'They're gone, all right,' he said; 'Swords, and red coats and pipeclay—they're gone. And a good riddance too! I should have been back before, only your ladies were talking, looking for you, so I had to wait till they were gone. I expect you'll want your dinner, sitting here so long? Well, cut and get it.'

He slung the boat rugs into a corner, blew out the lantern, and dropped a handful of snow on to the fire, 'Cut,' he continued. 'You can go. Get out of this. Run and get your dinners.' We went with him out of the hut into the square. 'See here,' he continued 'don't you go coming here. You don't know of this place—see? Don't you show your little tracks in this part of the wood; this is a private house, this is—trespassers will be prosecuted. Now run along and thank 'ee for your company.'

As Hugh began to squirm along the passage, I turned and shook hands with the man. I thought it would be the polite thing to do to say good-bye properly. 'Will you tell me your name?' I asked.

'Haven't got a name,' he answered gruffly. 'None of your business if I had.' He saw that I was hurt by his rudeness, for his face changed: 'I'll tell you,' he added quickly; 'but don't you say it about here. Gorsuch is my name—Marah Gorsuch.'

HUT IN THE GORSE-BUSHES 55

'Marah,' I said. 'What a funny name!'

'Is it?' he said grimly: 'It means bitter—bitter water, and I'm bitter on the tongue, as you may find. Now cut.'

'One thing more, Mr Gorsuch,' I said, 'be careful of your fires. They can smell them outside when the wind blows down from the wood.'

'Fires!' he exclaimed; 'I don't light fires here except I've little bleating schoolboys to tea. Cut and get your porridge. Here,' he called, as I went down on my hands and knees, 'here's a keepsake for you.'

He tossed me a little ornament of twisted silver wire woven into the form of a double diamond knot, probably by the man himself.

'Thank you, Mr Gorsuch,' I said.

'Oh, don't thank me,' he answered rudely: 'I'm tired of being thanked. Now cut.'

I wriggled through the clump after Hugh, then we ran home together through the wood, just as the dinner-bell was ringing for the second time.

Mrs Cottier asked us if we had not heard her calling.

'Yes, Mims,' I said, 'we did hear; but we were hidden in a secret house; we wondered if you would find us—we were close to you some of the time.'

My aunt said something about 'giving a lot of trouble' and 'being very thoughtless for others'; but we had heard similar lectures many times before and did not mind them much. After dinner I took Mims aside and told her everything; she laughed a little, though I could see that she was uneasy about Hugh.

'I wouldn't mention it to any one,' she said. 'It would be safer not. But oh, Jim, here we are, all three of us, in league with the law-breakers. The soldiers were here this morning asking all sorts of questions, and they'd two men prisoners with them, taken at Tor Cross on suspicion; they're to be sent to Exeter till the Assizes. I'm afraid it will go hard with them; I dare say they'll be sent abroad, poor fellows. Every house is being searched for last night's work: it seems they surprised the coastguards at the Cross and tied them up in their barracks, before they landed their goods, and now the whole country is being searched by troops. And here are we three innocents,' she went on, smiling, drawing us both to her, 'all

HUT IN THE GORSE-BUSHES 57

conspiring against the King's peace—I expect we shall all be transported. Well, I shall be transported, but you'd have to serve in the Navy. So now we won't talk about it any more; I've had enough smuggling for one day. Let's go out and build a real snow house, and then Jim will be a Red Indian and we will have a fight with bows and arrows.'

CHAPTER V

THE LAST VOYAGE OF 'THE SNAIL'

It was during the wintry days that Mrs Cottier decided to remove us from the school at Newton Abbot. She had arranged with the Rector at Strete for us to have lessons at the Rectory every morning with young Ned Evans, the Rector's son; so when the winter holidays ended we were spared the long, cold drive and that awful 'going back' to the school we hated so.

Winter drew to an end and the snow melted. March came in like a lion, bringing so much rain that the brook was flooded. We saw no more of the night-riders after that day in the snow, but we noticed little things now and then among the country people which made us sure that they were not far off. Once, when we were driving home in the evening after a day at Dartmouth, owls called along the road from just behind the hedge, whenever the road curved.

Hugh and I remembered the pheasants that day in the wood, and we nudged each other in the darkness, wondering whether Mr Gorsuch was one of the owls. After that night we used to practise the call of the owls and the pheasants, but we were only clever at the owl's cry: the pheasant's call really need's a man's voice, it is too deep a note for any boy to imitate well; but we could cry like the owls after some little practice, and we were very vain when we made an owl in the wood reply to us. Once, at the end of February, we gave the owl's cry outside the 'Adventure Inn,' where the road dips from Strete to the sands, and a man ran out to the door and looked up and down, and whistled a strange little tune, or scrap of a tune, evidently expecting an answer; but that frightened us; we made him no answer, and presently he went in muttering. He was puzzled, no doubt, for he came out again a minute later and again whistled his tune, though very quietly. We learned the scrap of tune and practised it together whenever we were sure that no one was near us.

As for the two men taken by the troops, they were let off. The innkeeper at South

Poole swore that both men had been in his inn all the night of the storm playing the 'ring-quoits' game with the other guests and as his oath was supported by half-a-dozen witnesses, the case for the King fell through; the night-riders never scrupled to commit perjury. Later on I learned a good deal about how the night-riders managed things.

During that rainy March, while the brook was in flood all over the valley, Hugh and I had a splendid time sailing toy boats, made out of boxes and pieces of plank. We had one big ship made out of a long wooden box which had once held flowers along a window-sill. We had painted ports upon her sides, and we had rigged her with a single square sail. With a strong south-westerly wind blowing up the valley, she would sail for nearly a mile whenever the floods were out, and though she often ran aground, we could always get her off, as the water was so shallow.

Now, one day (I suppose it was about the middle of the month) we went to sail this ship (we used to call her the *Snail*) from our side of the flood, right across the river-course, to the old slate quarry on the opposite side. The distance was, perhaps, three

LAST VOYAGE OF 'THE SNAIL' 61

hundred yards. We chose this site because in this place there was a sort of ridge causeway leading to a bridge, so that we could follow our ship across the flood without getting our feet wet. In the old days the quarry carts had crossed the brook by this causeway, but the quarry was long worked out, and the road and bridge were now in a bad state, but still good enough for us, and well above water.

We launched the *Snail* from a green, shelving bank, and shoved her off with the long sticks we carried. The wind caught her sail and drove her forward in fine style; she made a great ripple as she went. Once she caught in a drowned bush; but the current swung her clear, and she cut across the course of the brook like a Falmouth Packet. Hugh and I ran along the causeway, and over the bridge, to catch her on the other side. We had our eyes on her as we ran, for we feared that she might catch, or capsize; and we were so intent upon our ship that we noticed nothing else. Now when we came to the end of the causeway, and turned to the right, along the shale and rubble tipped there from the quarry, we saw a man coming down the slope to the water, evidently bent on catching the *Snail* when she arrived. We could not see his face very clearly, for he wore a grey slouch-hat, and the brambles were so high just there that sometimes they hid him from us. He seemed, somehow, a familiar figure; and the thought flashed through me that it might be Mr Gorsuch.

'Come on, Hugh,' I cried, 'or she'll capsize on the shale. The water's very shallow, so close up to this side.'

We began to run as well as we could, over the broken stones.

'It's no good,' said Hugh. 'She'll be there before we are.'

We broke through a brake of brambles to a green space sloping to the flood. There was the *Snail*, drawn up, high and dry, on to the grass, and there was the man, sitting by her on a stone, solemnly cutting up enough tobacco for a pipe.

'Good morning, Mr Gorsuch,' I said.

'Why, it's young sweetheart,' he answered. 'Why haven't you got your nurses with you?' He filled his pipe and lighted it, watching us with a sort of quizzical interest, but mak-

LAST VOYAGE OF 'THE SNAIL'

ing no attempt to shake hands. He made me feel that he was glad to see us; but that nothing would make him show it. 'What d'ye call this thing?' he asked, pointing with his toe to the *Snail*.

'That's our ship,' said Hugh.

'Is it?' he asked contemptuously. 'I thought it was your mother's pudding-box, with some of baby's bed-clothes on it. That's what I thought it was.'

He seemed to take a pleasure in seeing Hugh's face fall. Hugh always took a rough word to heart, and he could never bear to hear his mother mentioned by a stranger.

'It's a good enough ship for us,' he answered hotly.

'How d'ye know it is?' said the man. 'You know nothing at all about it. What do *you* know of ships, or what's good for you? Hey? You don't know nothing of the kind.'

This rather silenced Hugh; we were both a little abashed, and so we stood sheepishly for a moment looking on the ground.

At last I took Hugh by the arm. 'Let's take her somewhere else,' I said softly. I bent down and picked up the ship and turned to go.

The man watched us with a sort of amused contempt. 'Where are you going now?' he asked.

'Down the stream,' I called back.

'Drop it,' he said. 'Come back here.'

I called softly to Hugh to run. 'Shan't!' I cried as we started off together, at our best speed.

'Won't you?' he called. 'Then I'll make you.' He was after us in a brace of shakes, and had us both by the collar in less than a dozen yards. 'What little tempers we have got,' he said grinning. 'Regular little spitfires, both of you. Now back you come till we have had a talk.'

I noticed then that he was much better dressed than formerly. His clothes were of the very finest sea-cloth, and well cut. The buttons on his scarlet waistcoat were new George guineas; and the buttons on his coat were of silver, very beautifully chased. His shoes had big silver buckles on them, and there was a silver buckle to the flap of his grey slouch hat. The tattoo marks on his left hand were covered over by broad silver rings of the sort the Spanish onion-boys used to sell in Dartmouth, after the end of the war. He looked extremely handsome in his fine clothes. I wondered how I could ever have been afraid of him.

'Yes,' he said with a grin, when he saw me eyeing him, 'my ship came home all right. I was able to refit for a full due. So now we'll see what gifts the Queen sent.'

We wondered what he meant by this sentence; but we were not kept long in doubt. He led us through the briars to the ruins of the shed where the quarry overseer had formerly had his office.

'Come in here,' he said, shoving us in front of him, 'and see what the Queen 'll give you. Shut your eyes. That's the style. Now open.'

When we opened our eyes we could hardly keep from shouting with pleasure. There, on the ground, kept upright by a couple of bricks was a three-foot model of a revenue cutter, under all her sail except the big square foresail, which was neatly folded upon her yard. She was perfect aloft, even to her pennant; and on deck she was perfect too, with beautiful little model guns, all brass, on their carriages, pointing through the port holes.

'Oh' we exclaimed. 'Oh! Is she really for us, for our very own?'

'Why, yes,' he said. 'At least she's for you, Mr What's-your-name. Jim, I think you call yourself. Yes, Jim. Well, she's for you, Jim. I got something else the Queen sent for Mr Preacher feller.' He bent in one corner of the ruin, and pulled out what seemed to be a stout but broken box. 'This is for you, Mr Preacher feller,' he said to Hugh.

We saw that it was a model of a port of a ship's deck and side. The side was cut for a gun-port, which opened and shut by means of laniards; and, pointing through the opened port was a model brass nine-pounder on its carriage, with all its roping correctly rigged, and its sponges and rammers hooked up above it ready for use. It was a beautiful piece of work (indeed, both models were) for the gun was quite eighteen inches long. 'There you are,' said Marah Gorsuch. 'That lot's for you, Mr Preacher-feller. Them things is what the Queen sent.'

We were so much delighted by these beautiful presents that it was some minutes before we could find words with which to thank him. We could not believe that such things were really for us. He was much pleased to find that his gifts gave so much pleasure; he kept up a continual grin while we examined the toys inch by inch.

'Like 'em, hey?' he said.

'Yes; I should just think we do,' we answered. We shook him by the hand, almost unable to speak from pleasure.

'And now let's come down and sail her,' I said.

'Hold on there,' said Marah Gorsuch. 'Don't be too quick. You ain't going to sail that cutter till you know how. You've got a lot to learn first, so that must wait. It's to be Master Preacher-feller's turn this morning. Yours 'll come by-and-by. What you got to do, first go off, is to sink that old hulk you were playing with. We'll sink her at anchor with Preacher-feller's cannon.'

He told Hugh to pick up his toy, and to come along down to the water's edge. When he came near to the water, Marah took the old *Snail* and tied a piece of string to her bows by way of a cable. Then he thrust her well out into the flood, tied a piece of shale (as an anchor) to the other end of the string, and flung it out ahead of her, so that she rode at anchor trimly a few yards from the bank. 'Now,' he said, 'we'll exercise great guns. Here' (he produced a powder horn) 'is the magazine; here' (he produced a bag of bullets) 'is the shot-locker. Here's a bag of wads. Now, my sons, down to business. Cast loose your housings, take out tompions. Now bear a hand, my lads; we'll give your old galleon a broadside.'

We watched him as he prepared the gun for firing, eagerly lending a hand whenever we saw what he wanted. 'First of all,' he said, 'you must sponge your gun. There's the sponge. Shove it down the muzzle and give it a screw round. There! Now tap your sponge against the muzzle to knock the dust off. There! Now the powder.' He took his powder-horn and filled a little funnel (like the funnels once used by chemists for filling bottles of cough-mixture) with the powder. This he poured down the muzzle of the gun. 'Now a wad,' he said, taking up a screw of twisted paper. 'Ram it home on to the powder with the rammer. That's the way. Now for the shot. We'll put in a dozen bullets, and then top with a couple more wads. There! Now she's loaded. Those bullets will go for fifty yards with that much powder ahind 'em. Now, all we have to do is to prime her.' He filled the touch-hole with powder, and poured a few grains along the base or breech of the gun. 'There!' he said. 'Only one thing more. That is aim. Here, Mr. Preacher-feller, Hugh, whatever your name is. You're captain of the gun; you must aim her. Take a squint along the gun till you get the notch on the muzzle against the target; then raise your gun's breech till the notch is a little below your target. Those wooden quoins under the gun will keep it raised if you pull them out a little.'

Hugh lay down flat on the grass and moved the gun carefully till he was sure the aim was correct. 'Let's have a match,' he said, 'to see which is the best shot.'

'All right,' said Marah. 'We will. You have first shot. Are you ready? All ready? Very well then. Here's the linstock that you're to fire with.' He took up a long stick which had a slow match twisted round it. He lit the slow match by a pocket flint and steel after moving his powder away from him.

'Now then,' he cried, 'are you ready? Stand clear of the breech. Starboard battery. Fire!'

Hugh dropped the lighted match on to the priming. The gun banged loudly, leaped back and up, and fell over on one side in spite of its roping as the smoke spurted. At the same instant there was a lashing noise, like rain, upon the water as the bullets skimmed along upon the surface. One white splinter flew from the *Snail's* stern where a single bullet struck; the rest flew wide astern of her.

'Let your piece cool a moment,' said Marah, 'then we will sponge and load again, and then Jim 'll try. You were too much to the right, Mr Hugh. Your shots fell astern.'

After a minute or two we cleaned the gun thoroughly and reloaded.

'Now,' said Marah, 'remember one thing. If you was in a ship, fighting that other ship, you wouldn't want just to blaze away at her broadside. No. You'd want to hit her so as your shot would rake all along her decks from the bow aft, or from the stern forward. You wait a second, Master Jim, till the wind gives her bows a skew towards you, or till her stern swings round more. There she goes. Are you ready? Now, as she comes round; allow for it. Fire!'

LAST VOYAGE OF 'THE SNAIL'

Very hurriedly I made my aim, and still more hurriedly did I give fire. Again came the bang and flash; again the gun clattered over; but, to my joy, a smacking crack showed that the shot went home. The shock made the old *Snail* roll. A piece of her bow was knocked off. Two or three bullets ripped through her sail. One bored a groove along her, and the rest went over her.

'Good,' said Marah. 'A few more like that and she's all our own. Now it's my shot. I'll try to knock her rudder away. Wait till she swings. There she comes! There she comes! Over a little. Up a little. Now. Fire.' He darted his linstock down upon the priming. The gun roared and upset; the bullets banged out the *Snail's* stern, and she filled slowly, and sank to the level of the water, her mast standing erect out of the flood, and her whole fabric swaying a little as the water moved her up and down.

After that we fired at the mast till we had knocked it away, and then we placed our toys in the sheltered fireplace of the ruin and came away, happy to the bone, talking nineteen to the dozen.

CHAPTER VI

THE OWL'S CRY

For the next month we passed all our afternoons with Marah. In the mornings the Rector gave us our lessons at Strete; then we walked home to dinner; then we played with our gun and cutter, or at the sailing of our home-made boats, till about six, when we went home for tea. After tea we prepared our lessons for the next day, and went upstairs to bed, where we talked of smugglers and pirates till we fell asleep. Marah soon taught us how to sail the cutter; and, what was more, he taught us how to rig her. For an hour of each fine afternoon he would give us a lesson in the quarry office, showing us how to rig model boats, which we made out of old boxes and packing-cases. In the sunny evenings of April we used to sail our fleets, ship against ship, upon the great fresh-water lake into which the trout-brook

THE OWL'S CRY 73

passes on its way to the sea. Sometimes we would have a fleet of ships of the line anchored close to the shore, and then we would fire at them with the gun and with one of Marah's pistols till we had shattered them to bits and sunk them. Sometimes Marah would tell us tales of the smugglers and pirates of long ago, especially about a pirate named Van Horn, who was burned in his ship off Mugeres Island, near Campeachy, more than a hundred years back.

'His ship was full of gold and silver,' said Marah. 'You can see her at a very low tide even now. I've seen her myself. She is all burnt to a black coal, a great Spanish galleon, with all her guns in her. I was out fishing in the boat, and a mate said, "Look there. There she is!" and I saw her as plain as plain among all the weeds in the sea. The water's very clear there, and there she was, with the fishes dubbing their noses on her. And she's as full of gold as the Bank of England. The seas'll have washed Van Horn's bones white, and the bones of his crew too; eaten white by the fish and washed white, lying there in all that gold under the sea, with the weeds growing over them. It gives you a turn to think of it, don't it?'

'Why don't they send down divers to get the gold?' asked Hugh.

'Why,' said Marah. 'There's many has tried after all that gold. But some the sharks took and some the Spaniards took, and then there was storms and fighting. None ever got a doubloon from her. But somebody'll have a go for it again. I tried once, long ago. That was an unlucky try, though. Many poor men died along of that one. They died on the decks,' he added. 'It was like old Van Horn cursing us. They died in my arms, some of 'em. Seven and twenty seamen, and one of them was my mate, Charlie!'

I have wandered away from my story, I'm afraid, remembering these scraps of the past; but it all comes back to me now, so clearly that it seems to be happening again. There are Marah and Hugh, with the sun going down behind the gorse-bank, across the Lee; and there are the broken ships floating slowly past, with the perch rising at them; and there is myself, a very young cub, ignorant of what was about to come

THE OWL'S CRY

upon me. Perhaps, had I known what was to happen before the leaves of that spring had fallen, I should have played less lightheartedly, and given more heed to Mr Evans, the Rector.

Now, on one day in each week, generally on Thursdays, we had rather longer school hours than on the other days. On these days of extra work Hugh and I had dinner at the Rectory with Ned Evans, our schoolmate. After dinner we three boys would wander off together, generally down to Blackpool, where old Spanish coins (from some forgotten wreck) were sometimes found in the sand after heavy weather had altered the lie of the beach. We never found any Spanish coins, but we always enjoyed our afternoons there. The brook which runs into the sea there was very good for trout, in the way that Marah showed us; but we never caught any, for all our pains. In the summer we meant to bathe from the sands, and all through that beautiful spring we talked of the dives we would take from the spring-board running out into the sea. Then we would have great games of ducks and drakes, with flat pebbles; or games of pebble-dropping, in which our aim was to drop a stone so that it should make no splash as it entered the water. But the best game of all was our game of cliff-exploring among the cliffs on each side of the bay, and this same game gave me the adventure of my life.

One lovely afternoon towards the end of the May of that year, when we were grubbing among the cliff-gorse as usual, wondering how we could get down the cliffs to rob the sea-birds' nests, we came to a bare patch among the furze, and there lay a couple of coast-guards, looking intently at something a little further down the slope, and out of sight, beyond the brow of the cliff. They had ropes with them, and a few iron spikes, and one of them had his telescope on the grass beside him. They looked up at us angrily when we broke through the thicket upon them, and one of them hissed at us through his teeth: 'Get out, you boys. Quick. Cut!' and waved to us to get away, which we did, a good deal puzzled and perhaps a little startled. We talked about it on our way home. Ned Evans said that the men were setting rabbit snares, and that he had seen the wires. Hugh thought that they might be after sea-birds' eggs during their hours of duty. Both excuses seemed plausible, but for my own part I thought something very different. The men, I felt, were out on some special service, and on the brink of some discovery. It seemed to me that when we broke in upon them they were craning forward to the brow of the cliff, intently listening. I even thought that from below the brow of the cliff, only a few feet away, there had come a noise of people talking. I did not mention my suspicions to Hugh and Ned, because I was not sure, and they both seemed so sure; but all the way home I kept thinking that I was right. It flashed on me that perhaps the night-riders had a cave below the cliff-brow, and that the coastguards had discovered the secret. It was very wrong of me, but my only thought was: 'Oh, will they catch Marah? Will poor Marah be sent to prison?' and the fear that our friend would be dragged off to gaol kept me silent as we walked.

When we came to the gate which takes you by a short cut to the valley and the shale quarry, I said that I would go home that way, while the others went by the road, and that we would race each other, walking, to see who got home first. They agreed to this, and set off together at a great rate; but as soon as they were out of sight behind the hedge I buckled my satchel to my shoulders and started running to warn Marah. It was all downhill to the brook, and I knew that I should find Marah there, for he had said that he was coming earlier than usual that afternoon to finish off a model boat which we were to sail after tea. I ran as I had never run before—I thought my heart would thump itself to pieces; but at last I got to the valley and saw Marah crossing the brook by the causeway. I shouted to him then and he heard me. I had no breath to call again, so I waved to him to come and then collapsed, panting, for I had run a good mile across country. He walked towards me slowly, almost carelessly; but I saw that he was puzzled by my distress, and wondered what the matter was.

'What is it?' he asked. 'What's the rally for?'

'Oh,' I cried, 'the coastguards—over at Black Pool.'

'Yes,' he said carelessly, 'what about *them*?'

'They've discovered it,' I cried, 'The cave under the cliff-top. They've discovered it.'

His face did not change; he looked at me

THE OWL'S CRY

rather hard; and then asked me, quite carelessly, what I had seen.

'Two coastguards,' I answered. 'Two coastguards. In the furze. They were listening to people somewhere below them.'

'Yes,' he said, still carelessly, 'over at Black Pool? I suppose they recognized you?'

'Yes, they must have. We three are known all over the place. And I ran to tell you.'

'So I see,' he said grimly. 'You seem to have run like a tea-ship. Well, you needn't have. There's no cave on this side Salcombe, except the hole at Tor Cross. What made you run to tell *me*?'

'Oh,' I said, 'you've been so kind—so kind, and—I don't know—I thought they'd send you to prison.'

'Did you?' he said gruffly. 'Did you indeed? Well, they won't. There was no call for you to fret your little self. Still, you've done it; I'll remember that—I'll always remember that. Now you be off to your tea, quick. Cut!'

When he gave an order it was always well for us to obey it at once; if we did not he used to lose his temper. So when he told me to go I got up and turned away, but slowly, for I was still out of breath. I looked back before I passed behind the hedge which marks the beginning of the combe, but Marah had disappeared—I could see no trace of him. Then suddenly, from somewhere behind me, out of sight, an owl called—and this in broad daylight. Three times the 'Too-hoo, too-hoo' rose in a long wail from the shrubs, and three times another owl answered from up the combe, and from up the valley, too, till the place seemed full of owls. 'Too-hoo, too-hoo' came the cries, and very faintly came answers —some of them in strange tones, as though the criers asked for information. As they sounded, the first owl answered in sharp, broken cries. But I had had enough. Breathless as I was I ran on up the valley to the house, only hoping that no owl would come swooping down upon me. And this is what happened. Just as I reached the gate which leads to the little bridge below the house **I saw Joe Barn-coat** galloping towards me on an unsaddled horse of Farmer Rowser's. He seemed shocked, or upset, at seeing me; but he kicked the horse in the ribs and galloped on, crying out that he was having a little ride.

His little ride was taking him at a gallop to the owl, and I was startled to find that quiet Joe, the mildest gardener in the county, should be one of the uncanny crew whose signals still hooted along the combes.

When I reached home the others jeered at me for a sluggard. They had been at home for twenty minutes, and had begun tea. I let them talk as they pleased, and then settled down to work; but all that night I dreamed of great owls, riding in the dark with bee-skeps over them, filling the combes with their hootings.

CHAPTER VII

THE TWO COASTGUARDS

The next morning, when Hugh and I came to Strete for our lessons, we found a lot of yeomen and preventives drawn up in the village. People were talking outside their houses in little excited groups. Jan Edeclog, the grocer, was at the door of his shop, wiping his hands on his apron. There was a general rustle and stir, something had evidently happened.

'What's all the row about, Mr. Edeclog?' I asked.

'Row?' he asked. 'Row enough, Master Jim. Two of the coastguards who were on duty yesterday afternoon, have disappeared. It's thought there's been foul play.'

My heart sank into my boots, my head swam, I could hardly stand upright. All my thought was: 'They have been killed. And all through my telling Marah. And I'm a murderer.'

THE TWO COASTGUARDS 83

I don't know how I could have got to the Rectory gate, had not the militia captain come from the tavern at that moment. He mounted his horse, called out a word of command, and the men under him moved off towards Slapton at a quick trot.

'They have gone to beat the Lay banks,' said some one, and then some one laughed derisively.

I walked across to the Rectory and flung my satchel of books on to the floor. The Rector's wife came into the hall as we entered. 'Why, Jim,' she said, 'what *is* the matter? Aren't you well?'

'Not very,' I answered.

'My dear,' she cried to her husband, 'Jim's not well. He looks as though he'd seen a ghost, poor boy.'

'Why, Jim,' said the Rector, coming out of the sitting-room, 'what's the matter with you? Had too much jam for breakfast?'

'No,' I said. 'But I feel faint. I feel sick. Can I go to sit in the garden for a minute?'

'Yes,' he answered. 'Certainly. I'll get you a glass of cold water.'

I was really too far gone to pay much heed

to anything. I think I told them that I should be quite well in a few minutes, if they would leave me there; and I think that Mrs Evans told her husband to come indoors, leaving me to myself. At any rate they went indoors, and then the cool air, blowing on me from the sea, refreshed me, so that I stood up.

I could think of nothing except the words: 'I am a murderer.' A wild wish came to me to run to the cliffs by Black Pool to see whether the bodies lay on the grass in the place where I had seen them (full of life) only a few hours before. Anything was better than that uncertainty. In one moment a hope would surge up in me that the men would not be dead; but perhaps only gagged and bound: so that I could free them. In the next there would be a feeling of despair, that the men lay there, dead through my fault, killed by Marah's orders, and flung among the gorse for the crows and gulls. I got out of the Rectory garden into the road; and in the road I felt strong enough to run; and then a frenzy took hold of me, so that I ran like one possessed. It is not very far to Black Pool; but I think I ran the whole way. I didn't

THE TWO COASTGUARDS 85

feel out of breath when I got there, though I had gone at top speed; a spirit had been in me, such as one only feels at rare times. Afterwards, when I saw a sea-fight, I saw that just such a spirit filled the sailors, as they loaded and fired the guns.

I pushed my way along the cliffs through the gorse, till I came to the patch where the coastguards had lain. The grass was trampled and broken, beaten flat in places as though heavy bodies had fallen on it; there were marks of a struggle all over the patch. Some of the near-by gorse twigs were broken from their stems; some one had dropped a small hank of spunyarn. They had lain there all that night, for the dew was thick upon them. What puzzled me at first was the fact that there were marks from only two pairs of boots, both of the regulation pattern. The men who struggled with the coastguards must have worn moccasins, or heelless leather slippers, made out of some soft hide.

I felt deeply relieved when I saw no bodies, nor any stain upon the grass. I began to wonder what the night-riders had done with the coastguards; and, as I sat wondering, I heard, really and truly, a noise of the people talking from a little way below me, just beyond the brow of the cliff. That told me at once that there was a cave, even as I had suspected. I craned forward eagerly, as near as I dared creep, to the very rim of the land. I looked down over the edge into the sea, and saw the little blue waves creaming into foam far below me.

I could see nothing but the side of the cliff, with its projecting knobs of rock; no opening of any kind, and yet a voice from just below me (it seemed to come from below a little projecting slab a few feet down): a voice just below me, I say, said, quite clearly, evidently between puffs at a pipe, 'I don't know so much about that.' Another voice answered; but I could not catch the words. The voice I should have known anywhere; it was Marah's 'good-temper voice.' as he called it, making a pleasant answer.

'That settles it,' I said to myself. 'There's a cave, and the coastguards are there, I'll be bound, as prisoners. Now I have to find them and set them free.'

Very cautiously I peered over the cliff-face, examining every knob and ledge which might conceal (or lead to) an opening in the rock. No. I could see nothing; the cliff seemed to

THE TWO COASTGUARDS 87

me to be almost sheer; and though it was low tide, the rocks at the base of the cliffs seemed to conceal no opening. I crept cautiously along the cliff-top, as near to the edge as I dared, till I was some twenty feet from the spot where I had heard the voice. Then I looked down again carefully, searching every handbreadth for a firm foothold or path down the rocks, with an opening at the end, through which a big man could squeeze his body. No. There was nothing. No living human being could get down that cliff-face without a rope from up above; and even if he managed to get down, there seemed to be nothing but the sea for him at the end of his journey. Again I looked carefully right to the foot of the crag. No. There was absolutely nothing; I was off the track somehow.

Now, just at this point the cliff fell inland for a few paces, forming a tiny bay about six yards across. To get along the cliff towards Strete I had to turn inland for a few steps, then turn again to my left, and after a few more steps turn again towards the sea, in order to reach the cliff. I skirted the little bay in this manner, and dropped one or two stones into it from where I stood. As I craned over the edge, watching them fall into the sea, I caught sight of something far below me in the water.

I caught my breath and looked again, but the thing, whatever it was, had disappeared from sight. It was something red, which had gleamed for a moment from behind a rock at the base of the cliff. I watched eagerly for a moment or two, hearing the sucking of the sea along the stones, and the cry of the seagulls' young in their nests on the ledges. Then, very slowly, as the slack water urged it, I saw the red stem-piece of a rather large boat nosing slowly forward apparently from the cliff-face towards the great rock immediately in front of it. The secret was plain in a moment. Here was a cave with a sea-entrance, and a cave big enough to hide a large, sea-going fisher's boat; a cave, too, so perfectly hidden that it could not possibly be seen from any point except right at the mouth. A coastguard's boat could row within three yards of the entrance and never once suspect its being there, unless, at a very low tide, the sea clucked strangely from somewhere within. Any men entering the little bay in a boat would see only the big rock hiding the face of the cliff. No one would suspect that behind the rock lay a big cave accessible from the sea, at low tide in fair weather. Even in foul weather, good boatmen (and all the night-riders were wonderful fellows in a boat) could have made that cave in safety, for at the mouth of the little bay there was a great rock, which shut it in on the southwest side, so that in our bad south-westerly gales the bay or cove would have been sheltered, though full of the foam spattered from the sheltering crag.

I had found the cave, but my next task was to find an entrance, and that seemed to be no easy matter. I searched every inch of the cliff-face for a foothold, but there was nothing there big enough for anything bigger than a sea-lark. I could never have clambered down the cliff, even had I the necessary nerve, which I certainly had not. The only way down was to shut my eyes and walk over the cliff-edge, and trust to luck at the bottom, and 'that was one beyond me'—only Marah Gorsuch would have tried that way. No; there was no way down the cliff-side, that was certain.

Now, somebody—I think it was old Alec

Jewler, the ostler at the Tor Cross posting-house—had told me that here and there along the coast, but most of all in Cornwall, near Falmouth, there had once been arsenic mines, now long since worked out. Their shafts, he said, could be followed here and there for some little distance, and every now and again they would broaden out into chambers, in which people sometimes live, even now. It occurred to me that there might be some such shaft-opening among the gorse quite close to me; so I crept away from the cliff-brink, and began to search among the furze, till my skin was full of prickles. Though I searched diligently for an hour or two, I could find no hole big enough to be the mouth of a shaft. I knew that a shaft of the kind might open a hundred yards from where I was searching, and I was therefore well prepared to spend some time in my hunt. And at last, when I was almost tired of looking, I came across a fox or badger earth, not very recent, which seemed, though I could not be certain, to broaden out inside. I lay down and thrust my head down the hole, and that confirmed me. From up the hole there came the reek of strong ship's tobacco. I had stumbled upon one of the cave's air-holes.

CHAPTER VIII

THE CAVE IN THE CLIFF

My heart was thumping on my ribs as I thrust and wriggled my body down the hole. I did not think how I was to get back again; it never once occurred to me that I might stick in the burrow, and die stifled there, like a rat in a trap. My one thought was, 'I shall save the coastguards,' and that thought nerved me to push on, careless of everything else. It was not at all easy at first, for the earth fell in my ears from the burrow-roof, and there was very little room for my body. Presently, as I had expected, the burrow broadened out—I could kneel erect in it quite easily; and then I found that I could stand up without bumping my head. I was not frightened, I was only very excited; for, now that I stood in the shaft, the reek of the tobacco was very strong. I could see hardly anything —only the light from the burrow-mouth, lighting up the sides of the burrow for a yard or two, and a sort of gleam, a sort of shining wetness, upon the floor of the shaft and on its outer wall. I heard the wash of the sea, or thought I heard it, and that was the only noise, except a steady drip, drip, splash where water dripped from the roof into a pool on the floor. For a moment I stood still, not certain which way to go. Then I settled to myself the direction from which I had heard the voices, and turned along the shaft on that side.

When I had walked a few yards my nerve began to go; for the gleam on the walls faded, the last glimmer of light went out. I was walking along an unknown path in pitchy darkness, hearing only the drip, drip, splash of the water slowly falling from the roof. Suddenly I ran against a sort of breastwork of mortared stones, and the shock almost made me faint. I stretched my hand out beyond it, but could feel nothing, and then downward on the far side, but could feel nothing; and then I knocked away a scrap of stone from the top of the wall, and it seemed to fall for several seconds before a faint splash told me that it had reached water. The shaft seemed to turn to

the right and left at this low wall, and at first
I turned to the left, but only for a moment,
as I soon saw that the right-hand turning
would bring me more quickly to the cliff-
face from which I had heard the voices.

After I had made my choice, you may be
sure that I went on hands and knees, feeling
the ground in front of me. I went forward
very, very slowly, with the wet mud coming
through my knickerbockers, and the cold
drops sometimes falling on my neck from the
the roof. At last I saw a little glimmer of
light, and there was a turning to the left;
and just beyond the turning there was a chamber in the rock, all lit up by the sun, as clear
as clear. There were holes in the cliff-face,
one of them a great big hole, and the sun
shone through on to the floor of the cave, and
I could look out and see the sea, and the seagulls going past after fish, and the clouds
drifting up by the horizon. Very cautiously
I crept up to the entrance to the chamber,
and then into it, so that I could look all round
it.

It was not a very large room (I suppose it
was fifteen feet square) and it looked rather
smaller than it was, because it was heaped

almost to the roof in one or two places with boxes and kegs, and the various sea-stores, such as new rope and spare anchors. In one corner of it (in the corner at which I entered it) a flight of worn stone steps led downwards into the bowels of the earth. 'Aha!' I thought; 'so that's how you reach your harbour!' Then I crept up to one of the piles of boxes and cautiously peeped over.

I looked over cautiously, for as I entered the room I had the eerie feeling which one gets sometimes at night; I felt that there was somebody else in the room. Sure enough there was somebody else—two somebodies— and my heart leaped up in joy to see them. Sitting on the ground, tied by the body to some of the boxes over which I peered, were the two missing coastguards. Their backs were towards me, and their hands and feet were securely bound; but they were unhurt, that was the great thing. One of them was quietly smoking, filling the cave with strong tobacco smoke; the other was asleep, breathing rather heavily. It was evidently a pleasant holiday for the pair of them. No other person was in the room, but I saw that on the far side of the chamber another gallery led on into

THE CAVE IN THE CLIFF

the cliff to another chamber, and from this chamber came the sound of many voices talking (in a dull quiet way), and the slow droning of the song of a drunken man. I shut my eyes, and lay across the boxes as still as a dead man, trying to summon up enough courage to speak to the coastguard; and all the time the drunkard's song quavered and shook, and died down, and dragged on again, as though it would never end. Afterwards I often heard that song, in all its thirty stanzas; and I have only to repeat a line of it to bring back to myself the scene of the sunny cave, with the bound coastguard smoking, and the smugglers talking and talking just a few paces out of sight.

> 'And the gale it roar-ed dismally
> As we went to New Barbary,'

said the singer; and then some one asked a question, and some one struck a light for his pipe, and the singer droned on and on about the bold Captain Glen, and the ship which met with such disaster.

At last I summoned up enough courage to speak. I crawled over the boxes as far as I could, and touched the coastguard. 'Sb!'

I said, in a low voice. 'Don't make a sound. I've come to rescue you.'

The man started violently (I dare say his nerves were in a bad way after his night in the cave), he dropped his pipe with a little clatter on the stones, and turned to stare at me.

'Sh!' I said again. 'Don't speak. Don't make a sound.'

I crept round the boxes to him, and opened my knife. It was a strong knife, with very sharp blades (Marah used to whet them for me), so that it did not take me long to cut through the 'inch-and-a-half-rope,' which lashed the poor fellow to the boxes.

'Thankee, master,' the man said, as he rose to his feet and stretched himself. 'I was getting stiff. Now, let's get out of here. D'ye know the way out?'

'Yes,' I said, 'I think I do. Oh, don't make a noise; but come this way. This way.'

Very quietly we stole out by the gallery by which I had entered. We made no attempt to rouse the sleeping man; he slept too heavily, and we could not afford to run risks. I don't know what the coastguard's feelings were. As for myself, I was pretty nearly fainting with

THE CAVE IN THE CLIFF

excitement. I could hear my heart go thump, thump, thump; it seemed to be right up in my very throat. As we stepped into the gloom of the gallery, the smugglers behind us burst into the chorus at the end of the song—

> 'O never more do I intend
> For to cross the raging main
> But to live at home most cheerfull-ee,
> And thus I end my traged-ee.'

I felt that if I could get away from that adventure, I too, would live at home most cheerfully until the day of my death. We took advantage of the uproar to step quickly into the darkness of the passage.

Just before we came to the low stone breastwork which had given me such a shock a few minutes before, we heard some one whistling a bar of a tune. The tune was the tune of—

'Oh, my true love's listed, and wears a white cockade.'

And to our horror the whistler was coming quickly towards us. In another second we saw him stepping along the gallery, swinging a lantern. He was a big, strong man, evidently familiar with the way.

'Back,' said the coastguard in a gasp. 'Get back, for your life, and down that staircase.'

The man didn't see us; didn't even hear us. He stopped at the stone breastwork, opened his lantern, and lit his pipe at the candle, and then stepped on leisurely towards the chamber. Our right course would have been 'to go for him,' knock him down, knock the breath out of him, lash his wrists and ankles together, and bolt for the entrance. But the coastguard was rather upset by his adventure, and he let the minute pass by. Had he rushed at the man as soon as he appeared; but, there —it is no use talking. We didn't rush at him, we scuttled back into the chamber, and then down the worn stone steps cut out of the rock, which seemed to lead down and down into the bowels of the earth. As we hurried down, leaping lightly on the tips of our toes, the quaver of the tune came after us, so clearly that I even made a guess at the whistler's identity.

When we had run down the staircase about half-way down to sea-level we found ourselves in a cave as big as the church at Dartmouth. It was fairly light, for the entrance was large,

THE CAVE IN THE CLIFF 99

though low, and at low water (as it was then) the roof of the cave mouth stood six feet from the sea. The sea ran up into the cave in a deep triangular channel, with a landing-place (a natural ledge of rock) on each of the sides, and the sea entrance at the base. The sea made a sort of clucking noise about the rocks; and at the right inland it washed upon a cave-floor of pebbles, which clattered slightly as the swell moved them. The roof dripped a little, and there were little pools on both the landings, and the whole place had a queer, dim, green, uncanny light upon it; due, I suppose, to the deep water of the channel. I saw all these things afterwards, at leisure; I did not notice them very clearly in that first moment. All that I saw then was a large sea-lugger, lying moored at the cave-mouth, some few feet lower down. She was a beautiful model of a boat (I had seen that much in seeing her bow from the top of the cliff), but of course her three masts were unstepped, and she was rather a handful for a man and a boy. We saw her, and made a leap for her together, and both of us landed in her bows at the same instant, just as the man with the lantern, peering down from the top of the stairs, asked us what in the world we were playing at down there.

The coastguard made no answer, for he was busy in the bows; I think he had his knife through the painter in five seconds. Then he snatched up a boat-hook (I took an oar), and we drove her with all our strength along the channel into (or, I should say, towards) the open sea and freedom.

'Hey,' cried the man with the lantern, 'chuck that! Are you mad?' He took a step or two down the staircase, in order to see better.

'Drive her, oh, drive her, boy!' cried the coastguard.

I thrust with all my force, the coastguard gave a mighty heave, the lugger slid slowly seawards.

'Hey!' yelled the smuggler, clattering upstairs, dropping his lantern down on us. 'Hey, Marah, Fowler, Smokewell, Harkin—all of you! They've got away in the boat.'

'Now the play begins,' said the coastguard. 'Another heave, and another—together now!'

We drove the lugger forward again, so that half her length thrust out into the sea. We ran aft to give her a final thrust out, and just

THE CAVE IN THE CLIFF 101

at that moment her bow struck upon the rock at the cave mouth: in the excitement of the moment we had not realised that one of us was wanted in the bows to shove her nose clean into the sea. The blow threw us both upon our hands and knees in the stern sheets; it took us half-a-dozen seconds to pick ourselves up, and then I realised that I should have to jump forward and guide the boat clear of all outlying dangers. As I sprang to the bows there came yells from the top of the stairs, where I saw half-a-dozen smugglers coming full tilt towards us.

Some one cried out 'Drop it, drop it, you fool!' Another voice cried 'Fire!' and two or three shots cracked out, making a noise like a cannonade. The coastguard gave a last desperate heave, I shoved the bows clear, and lo! we were actually gliding out. The coastguard's body was outside the cliff in full sunlight, giving a final thrust from the cliff wall. And then I saw Marah leap into the stern sheets as they passed out of the cave; he gave a little thrust to the coastguard, just a gentle thrust—enough to make him lose his balance and topple over.

'That's enough now,' he said, with a grim

glance at me. 'That's enough for one time.'

He picked up the coastguard's boat-hook (the man just grinned and looked sheepish; he made no attempt to fight with Marah) and thrust the boat back into the cave with half-a-dozen deft strokes. Another smuggler dropped down into the stern sheets, looked at the coastguard with a grin, and helped to work the lugger back into the cave. A third man threw down a sternfast to secure her; a fourth jumped into the bow and began to cut a long splice into the painter which we had cut. We had tried and we had failed; here we were prisoners again, and I felt sick at heart lest those rough smugglers should teach us a lesson for our daring. But Marah just told the coastguard to jump out.

'Out you get,' he said, 'and don't try that again.'

'I won't,' said the coastguard.

'You'd better not,' said another smuggler. That was all.

We were helped out of the lugger on to the ledge above the channel, and the smugglers walked behind us up the stairs to the room we had just left. The other coastguard was still snoring, and that seemed strange to me, for the last few minutes had seemed like hours.

'Better bring him inside, boss,' said one of the smugglers. 'He may try the same game.'

'He's got no young sprig to cut his lashings,' said Marah. 'He'll be well enough.' So they left the man to his quiet and passed on with their other prisoners into the inner room.

CHAPTER IX

SIGNING ON

The inner room was much larger than the prison chamber; it was not littered with boxes, but clean and open like a frigate's lower deck. It was not, perhaps, quite so light as the other room, but there were great holes in the cliff hidden by bushes from the view of passing fishermen, and the sun streamed through these on to the floor, leaving only the ends of the room in shadow. The room had been arranged like the mess-deck of a war-ship; there were sea-chests and bags ranged trimly round the inner wall; there was a trestle table littered with tin pannikins and plates. The roof was supported by a line of wooden stanchions. There were arm racks round the stanchions, containing muskets, cutlasses, and long, double-barrelled pistols. As I expected, there were several bee-skeps hanging from nails, or lying on the floor. I was in the smug-

SIGNING ON

glers' roost, perhaps in the presence of Captain Sharp himself.

The drunken smuggler who had sung of Captain Glen was the only occupant of the room when we entered: he sat half asleep in his chest, still clutching his pannikin, still muttering about the boatswain. He was an Italian by birth, so Marah told me. He was known as Gateo. When he was sober he was a good seaman, but when he was drunk he would do nothing but sing of Captain Glen until he dropped off to sleep. He had served in the Navy, Marah told me, and had once been a boatswain's mate in the *Victory;* but he had deserted, and now he was a smuggler living in a hole in the earth.

'And now,' said Marah, after he had told me all this, 'you and me will have to talk. Step into the other room there, you boys,' he cried to the other smugglers: 'I want to have a word with master here.'

One of the men—he was the big man who had raised the alarm on us; I never knew his real name, everybody always called him Extry—said glumly that he 'wasn't going to oblige boys, not for dollars.'

Marah turned upon him, and the two men

faced each other; the others stood expectantly, eager for a fight.

'Step into the other room there,' repeated Marah quietly.

'I ain't no pup nor no nigger-man,' said Extry. 'You ain't going to order me.'

Marah seemed to shrink into himself and to begin to sparkle all over—I can't describe it: that is the effect he produced—he seemed to settle down like a cat going to spring. Extry's hand travelled round for his sheath-knife, and yet it moved indecisively, as though half afraid. And then, just as I felt that Extry would die from being looked at in that way, he hung his head, turned to the door, and walked out sheepishly according to order. He was beaten.

'No listening now,' said Marah, as they filed out. 'Keep on your own side of the fence.'

'Shall we take Gatty with us?' said one of the men.

'Let him lie,' said Marah; 'he's hove down for a full due, Gatty is.'

The men disappeared with their prisoner. Marah looked after them for a moment. 'Now,' he said, 'come on over here to the

SIGNING ON

table, Master Jim.' He watched me with a strange grin upon his face; I knew that grin; it was the look his face always bore when he was worried. 'Now we will come to business. Lie back against the hammocks and rest; I'm going to talk to you like a father.'

I lay back upon the lashed-up hammocks and he began.

'I suppose you know what you've done? You've just about busted yourself. D'ye know that? You thought you'd rescue the pugs'—he meant coastguards. 'Well, you haven't. You have gone and shoved your head down a wasp's nest, so you'll find. How did you get here, in the first place? What gave you your clue?'

'I saw the coastguards up above here yesterday,' I answered, 'and I thought I heard voices speaking from below the brow of the cliff, so then I searched about till I found a hole, and so I got down here.'

'Ah,' said Marah, 'they will be round here looking for you, then. I'll take the liberty of hiding your tracks.' He went into the other room and spoke a few words to one of the other smugglers. 'Well,' he said, as he came back to me, 'they'll not find you now, if they search from now till glory. They'll think you fell into the sea.'

'But,' I exclaimed, 'I must go home! Surely I can go home now? They'll be so anxious.'

'Yes,' said Marah, 'they'll be anxious. But look you here, my son; folk who acts hasty, as you've done, they often make other people anxious—often enough. Very anxious indeed, some of 'em. That's what you have done by coming nosing around here. Now here you are, our prisoner—Captain Sharp's prisoner—and here you must stay.'

'But, I *must* go home,' I cried, the tears coming to my eyes. 'I *must* go home.'

'Well, you just can't,' he answered kindly. 'Think it over a minute. You've come here,' he went on, 'nosing round like a spy; you've found out our secret. You might let as many as fifty men in for the gallows—fifty men to be hanged, d'ye understand; or to be transported, or sent to a hulk, or drafted into a man-o'-war. I don't say you would, for I believe you have sense; still, you're only a boy, and they might get at you in all sorts of ways. Cunning lawyers might. And then you'd give us away and where would *we* be? Eh, boy? Where would we be? Suppose you gave us away, meaning no harm, not really knowing what you done. Well, I ask you, where would *we* be?'

'I wouldn't give you away,' I said hotly. 'You know I wouldn't. I never gave you away about the hut in the woods.'

'No,' he said, 'you never; but this time there's men's necks concerned. I can't help myself—Captain Sharp's orders. I couldn't let you go if I wanted to; the hands wouldn't let me. It'd be putting so many ropes round their necks.' By this time I was crying. 'Don't cry young 'un,' he said; 'it won't be so bad. But you see yourself what you've done now, don't you?'

He walked away from me a turn or two to let me have my cry out. When my sobs ceased, he came back and sat close to me, waiting for me to speak.

'What will you do to me?' I asked him.

'Why,' he answered, 'there's only one thing *to* be done; either you've got to become one of us, so as if you give us away you'll be in the same boat—I don't say you need be one of us for long; only a trip or two—or, you'll have to walk through the window there, and that's a long fall and a mighty wet splash at the bottom.'

I thought of Mims waiting at home for me, and of the jolly tea-table, with Hooly begging for toast and Hugh's face bent over his plate. The thought that I should never see them again set me crying passionately—I cried as if my heart would break.

'Why—come, come,' said Marah; 'I thought you were a sailor. Take a brace, boy. We're not going to kill you. You'll make a trip or two. What's that? Why it's only a matter of a week or two, and it'll make a man of you. A very jolly holiday. I'll be able to make a man of you just as I said I would. You'll see life and you'll see the sea, and then you'll come home and forget all about us. But go home you'll not, understand that, till we got a hold on you the same as you on us.'

There was something in his voice which gave me the fury of despair. I sprang to my feet, almost beside myself. 'Very well, then,' I cried. 'You can drown me. I'm not going to be one of you. And if I ever get away I'll see you all hanged, every one of you—you first.'

I couldn't say more, for I burst out crying again.

SIGNING ON   111

Marah sat still, watching me. 'Well, well,' he said, 'I always thought you had spirit. Still, no sense in drowning you, no sense at all.'

He walked to the door and called out to some of the smugglers, 'Here, Extry, Hankin, you fellows, just come in here, I want you a moment.'

The men came in quickly, and ranged themselves about the room, grinning cheerfully.

''Low me to introduce you,' said Marah. 'Our new apprentice, Mr Jim Davis.'

The men bowed to me sheepishly.

'Glad to meet Mr Davis,' said one of them.

'Quite a pleasure,' said another.

'I s'pose you just volunteered, Mr Jim?' said the third.

'Yes,' said Marah; 'he just volunteered. I want you to witness his name on the articles.' He produced a sheet of paper which was scrawled all over with names. 'Now, Mr Jim,' he said, 'your name, please. There's ink and pen in the chest here.'

'What d'ye want my name for?' I asked.

'Signing on,' he said, winking at me. It's only a game.'

'I won't set my name to the paper.' I

cried. 'I'll have nothing to do with you. I'd sooner die—far sooner.'

'That's a pity,' said Marah, taking up the pen. 'Well, if you won't, you won't.'

He bent over the chest and wrote 'Jim Davis' in a round, unformed, boyish hand, not unlike my own.

'Now, lads', he said, 'you have seen the signature. Witness it, please.'

The men witnessed the signature and made their clumsy crosses; none of them could write.

'You see?' asked Marah. 'We were bound to get you, Jim. You've signed our articles.'

'I've done nothing of the kind,' I said.

'Oh! but you have,' he said calmly. 'Here's your witnessed signature. You're one of us now.'

'It's a forgery!' I cried.

'Forgery?' he said in pretended amazement. 'But here are witnesses to swear to it. Now don't take on, son'—he saw that I was on the point of breaking down again at seeing myself thus trapped. 'You can't get away. You're ours. Make the best of a bad job. We will tell your friends you are safe. They'll know within an hour that you will

SIGNING ON

not be home till the end of June. After that you will be enough one of us to keep your tongue shut for your own sake. I'm sorry you don't like it. Well, "The sooner the quicker" is a good proverb. The sooner you dry your tears, the quicker we can begin to work together. Here Smokewell, get dinner along; it's pretty near two o'clock. Now, Jim, my son, I'll just send a note to your people.' He sat down on a chest and began to write. 'No', he added; '*you* had better write. Say this: "I am safe. I shall be back in three weeks' time. Say I have gone to stay in Somersetshire with Captain Sharp. Do not worry about me. Do not look for me. I am safe." There; that's enough. Give it here. Hankin, deliver this letter at once to Mrs Cottier, at the Snail's Castle. Don't show your beautiful face to more'n you can help. Be off.'

Hankin took the letter and shambled out of the cave. Long afterwards I heard that he shot it through the dining-room window on a dart of hazelwood while the aunt and Mrs Cottier were at lunch. That was the last letter I wrote for many a long day. That was my farewell to boyhood, that letter.

After a time Smokewell brought in dinner, and we all fell-to at the table. For my own part, I was too sick at heart to eat much, though the food was good enough. There was a cold fowl, a ham, and a great apple-pasty.

After dinner, the men cut up tobacco, and played cards, and smoked, and threw dice; but Marah made them do this in the outer room. He was very kind to me in my wretchedness. He slung one of the hammocks for me, and made me turn in for a sleep. After a time I cried myself into a sort of uneasy doze. I woke up from time to time, and whenever I woke up I would see Marah smoking, with his face turned to the window, watching the sea. Then I would hear the flicker of the cards in the next room, and the voices of the players. 'You go that? Do you? Well, and I'll raise you.' And then I would hear the money being paid to the winners, and wonder where I was, and so doze off again into all manner of dreams.

CHAPTER X

ABOARD THE LUGGER

When I woke up, it was still bright day, but the sun was off the cliffs, and the caves seemed dark and uncanny.

'Well,' said Marah, 'have you had a good sleep?'

'Yes,' I said, full of wretchedness; 'I must have slept for hours.'

'You'll need a good sleep,' said Marah, 'for it's likely you'll have none to-night. We night-riders, the like of you and me, why, we know what the owls do, don't we? We sleep like cats in the day-time. They'll be getting supper along in about half-an-hour. What d'you say to a wash and that down in the sea— a plunge in the cove and then out and dry yourself? Why it'd be half your life. Do you all the good in the world. Can't offer you fresh water; there's next to none down below here. But you come down and have a dip in the salt.'

He led the way into the next room, and down the stairs to the water. The tide was pretty full, so that I could dive off one ledge and climb out by the ledge at the other side. So I dived in and then climbed back, and dried myself with a piece of an old sail, feeling wonderfully refreshed. Then we went upstairs to the cave again, and supped off the remains of the dinner; and then the men sat about the table talking, telling each other stories of the sea. It was dusk before we finished supper, and the caves were dark, but no lights were allowed. The smugglers always went into the passages to light their pipes. I don't know how they managed in the winter: probably they lived in the passages, where a fire could not be seen from the sea. In summer they could manage very well.

Towards sunset the sky clouded over, and it began to rain. I sat at the cave window, listlessly looking out upon it, feeling very sick at heart. The talk of the smugglers rang in my ears in little snatches.

'So I said, "You're a liar. There's no man alive ever came away, not ever. They were all drowned, every man Jack." That's what I said.'

ABOARD THE LUGGER

'Yes,' said another; 'so they was. I saw the wreck myself. The lower masts was standing.'

I didn't understand of half what they said; but it all seemed to be full of terrible meaning, like the words heard in dreams. Marah was very kind in his rough sailor's way, but I was homesick, achingly homesick, and his jokes only made me more wretched than I was. At last he told me to turn in again and get some sleep, and, after I had tucked myself up, the men were quieter. I slept in a dazed, light-headed fashion (as I had slept in the afternoon), till some time early in the morning (at about one o'clock), when a hand shook my hammock, and Marah's voice bade me rise.

It was dark in the cave, almost pitch-dark. Marah took my arm and led me downstairs to the lower cave, where one or two battle-lanterns made it somewhat lighter. There were nearly twenty men gathered together in the cave, and I could see that the lugger had been half filled with stores, all securely stowed, ready for the sea. A little, brightly-dressed mannikin, in a white, caped overcoat, was directing matters, talking sometimes in English, sometimes in French, but always with a refined accent and in picked phrases. He was clean shaven, as far as I could see, and his eyes glittered in the lantern-light. The English smugglers addressed him as Captain Sharp, but I learnt afterwards that 'Captain Sharp' was the name by which all their officers were known, and that there were at least twenty other Captain Sharps scattered along the coast. At the time, I thought that this man was the supreme head, the man who had sent Mrs Cottier her present, the man who had spoken to me that night of the snow-storm.

'Here, Marah,' he said, when he saw that I was taking too much notice of him, 'stow that lad away in the bows; he will be recognising me by-and-by.'

'Come on, Jim,' said Marah; 'jump into the boat, my son.'

'But where are we going?' I asked, dismayed.

'Going?' he answered. 'Going? Going to make a man of you. Going to France, my son.'

I hung back, frightened and wretched. He swung me lightly off the ledge into the lugger's bows.

'Now, come,' he said; 'you're not going to

ABOARD THE LUGGER 119

cry. I'm going to make a man of you. Here, you must put on this suit of wrap-rascal, and these here knee-boots, or you'll be cold to the bone, 'specially if you're sick. Put 'em on, son, before we sail.' He didn't give me time to think or to refuse, but forced the clothes upon me; they were a world too big. 'There,' he said; 'now you're quite the sailor.' He gave a hail to the little dapper man above him. 'We're all ready, Captain Sharp,' he cried, 'so soon as you like.'

Right,' said the Captain. 'You know what you got to do. Shove off, boys!'

A dozen more smugglers leaped down upon the lugger; the gaskets were cast off the sails, a few ropes were flung clear. I saw one or two men coiling away the lines which had lashed us to the rocks. The dapper man waved his hands and skipped up the staircase.

'Good-bye, Jim,' said some one. 'So long—so long,' cried the smugglers to their friends. Half-a-dozen strong hands walked along the ledge with the sternfast, helping to drag us from the cave. 'Quietly now,' said Marah, as the lugger moved out into the night. 'Heave, oh, heave,' said the seamen, as they thrust her forward to the sea. The sea air beat freshly upon me, a drop or two of rain fell, wetting my skin, the water talked under the keel and along the cliff-edge—we were out of the cave, we were at sea; the cave and the cliff were a few yards from us, we were moving out into the unknown.

'Aft with the boy, out of the way,' said some one; a hand led me aft to the stern sheets, and there was Marah at the tiller. 'Get sail on her,' he said in a low voice.

The men ran to the yards and masts, the masts were stepped and the yards hoisted quietly. There was a little rattle of sheets and blocks, the sails slatted once or twice. Then the lugger past from the last shelter of the cliff; the wind caught us, and made us heel a little; the men went to the weather side; the noise of talking water deepened. Soon the water creamed into brightness as we drove through it. They set the little main topsail—luggers were never very strictly rigged in those days.

'There's the Start Light, Jim,' said Marah. 'Bid it good-bye. You'll see it no more for a week.'

They were very quiet in the lugger; no

one spoke, except when the steersman was relieved, or when the master wished something done among the rigging. The men settled down on the weather side with their pipes and quids, and all through the short summer night we lay there, huddled half asleep together, running to the south like a stag. At dawn the wind breezed up, and the lugger leaped and bounded till I felt giddy; but they shortened no sail, only let her drive and stagger, wasting no ounce of the fair wind. The sun came up, the waves sparkled, and the lugger drove on for France, lashing the sea into foam and lying along on her side. I didn't take much notice of things for I felt giddy and stunned; but the change in my circumstances had been so great—the life in the lugger was so new and strange to me—that I really did not feel keen sorrow for being away from my friends. I just felt stunned and crushed.

Marah was at the taffrail looking out over the water with one hand on the rail. He grinned at me whenever the sprays rose up and crashed down upon us. 'Ha,' he would say, 'there she sprays; that beats your shower-baths,' and he would laugh to see me duck whenever a very heavy spray flung itself into

'Who? James M'Kenna?' he answered lightly. 'He stole the admiral's pig. He was hanged at the yardarm until he was dead. You thank your stars we have not got far to go. There's France fair to leeward; but that cutter's between us and there, so we shall have a close call to get home. P'raps we shall not *get* home—it depends, my son.'

the boat. We were tearing along at a great pace and there were two men at the tiller: Marah was driving his boat in order to 'make a passage.' We leaped and shook, and lay down and rushed, like a thing possessed; our sails were dark with the spray; nearly every man on board was wet through.

By-and-by Marah called me to him and took me by the scruff of the neck with one hand. 'See here,' he said, putting his mouth against my ear; 'look just as though nothing was happening. You see that old Gateo at the lee tiller? Well, watch him for a moment. Now look beyond his red cap at the sea. What's that? Your eyes are younger—I use tobacco too much to have good eyes. What's that on the sea there?'

I looked hard whenever the lugger rose up

CHAPTER XI

THE FRIGATE 'LAOCOON'

By this time the other smugglers had become alarmed. The longboat gun, which worked on a slide abaft all, was cleared, and the two little cohorns, or hand-swivel guns, which pointed over the sides, were trained and loaded. A man swarmed up the mainmast to look around. 'The cutter's bearing up to close,' he called out. 'I see she's the Salcombe boat.'

'That shows they have information,' said Marah grimly, 'otherwise they'd not be looking for us here. Some one had been talking to his wife.' He hailed the masthead again. 'Have the frigates seen us yet?'

For answer, the man took a hurried glance to wind-ward, turned visibly white to the lips, and slid down a rope to the deck. 'Bearing down fast, under stunsails,' he reported. 'The cutter's signalled them with her topsail. There's three frigates coming down,' he added.

'Right,' said Marah. I'll go up and see for myself.'

THE FRIGATE 'LAOCOON' 125

He went up, and came down again looking very ugly. He evidently thought that he was in a hole. 'As she goes,' he called to the helmsman 'get all you can on the sheets, boys. Now Jim, you're up a tree; you're within an hour of being pressed into the Navy. How'd ye like to be a ship's boy, hey, and get tickled up by a bo'sun's rope-end?'

'I shouldn't like it at all,' I answered.

'You'll like it a jolly sight less than that,' said he, 'and it's what you'll probably be. We're ten miles from home. The cutter's in the road. The frigates will be on us in half-an-hour. It will be a mighty close call, my son; we shall have to fight to get clear.'

At that instant of time something went overhead with a curious whanging whine.

'That's a three-pound ball,' said Marah, pointing to a spurt upon a wave. 'The cutter wants us to stop and have breakfast with 'em.'

'Whang,' went another shot, flying far overhead. 'Fire away,' said Marah. You're more than a mile away; you will not hit us at that range.'

He shifted his course a little, edging more towards the shore, so as to cut transversely across the cutter's bows. We ran for twenty minutes in the course of the frigates; by that time the cutter was within half a mile and the frigates within three miles of us. All the cutter's guns were peppering at us; a shot or two went through our sails, one shot knocked a splinter from our fiferail.

'They shoot a treat, don't they?' said Marah. 'Another minute and they will be knocking away a spar.'

Just as he spoke, there came another shot from the cutter; something aloft went 'crack'; a rope unreeved from its pulley and rattled on to the deck; the mizen came down in a heap: the halliards had been cut clean through. The men leaped to repair the damage; it took but a minute or two, but we had lost way; the next shot took us square amidships and tore off a yard of our lee side.

'We must give them one in return,' he said. 'Aft to the gun, boys.'

The men trained the long gun on the cutter. 'Oh, Marah,' I said, 'don't fire on Englishmen.'

'Who began the firing?' he answered. 'I'm going to knock away some of their sails. Stand clear of the breach,' he shouted, as he pulled the trigger-spring.

THE FRIGATE 'LAOCOON'

The gun roared and recoiled; a hole appeared as if by magic in the swelling square foresail of the cutter. 'Load with bar-shot and chain,' said Marah. 'Another like that and we shall rip the whole sail off. Mind your eye. There goes her gun again.'

This time the shot struck the sea beside us, sending a spout of water over our rail. Again Marah pulled his trigger-string, the gun fell over on its side, and the cutter's mast seemed to collapse into itself as though it were wrapping itself up in its own canvas. A huge loose clue of sail—the foresail's starboard leach—flew up into the air; the boom swung after it; the gaff toppled over from above; we saw the topmast dive like a lunging rapier into the sea. We had torn the foresail in two, and the shot passing on had smashed the foremast just below the cap. All her sails lay in a confused heap just forward of the mast.

'That's done her,' said one of the smugglers. 'She can't even use her gun now.'

'Hooray!' cried another. 'We're the boys for a lark.'

'Are you?' said Marah. 'We got the frigates to clear yet, my son. They'll be in range in two minutes or less. Look at them.'

Tearing after us, in chase, under all sail, came the frigates. Their bows were burrowing into white heaps of foam; we could see the red portlids and the shining gun-muzzles; we could see the scarlet coats of the marines, and the glint of brass on the poops. A flame spurted from the bows of the leader. She was firing a shot over us to bid us heave to. The smugglers looked at each other; they felt that the game was up. Bang! Another shot splashed into the sea beside us, and bounded on from wave to wave, sending up huge splashes at each bound. A third shot came from the second frigate, but this also missed. Marah was leaning over our lee rail, looking at the coast of France, still several miles away. 'White water,' he cried suddenly. 'Here's the Green Stones. We shall do them yet.'

I could see no green stones, but a quarter of a mile away, on our port-hand, the sea was all a cream of foam above reefs and sands just covered by the tide. If they were to help us, it was none too soon, for by this time the leading frigate was only a hundred yards from us. Her vast masts towered over us. I could look into her open

THE FRIGATE 'LAOCOON' 129

bow ports; I could see the men at the bow guns waiting for the word to fire. I have often seen ships since then, but I never saw any ship so splendid and so terrible as that one. She was the *Laocoön*, and her figure-head was twined with serpents. The line of her ports was of a dull yellow colour, and as all her ports were open, the portlids made scarlet marks all along it. Her great lower studding sail swept out from her side for all the world like a butterfly-net, raking the top of the sea for us. An officer stood on the forecastle with a speaking-trumpet in his hand.

'Stand by!' cried Marah. 'They're going to hail us.'

'Ahoy, the lugger there!' yelled the officer. 'Heave too at once or I sink you. Heave to.'

'Answer him in French,' said Marah to one of the men.

A man made some answer in French; I think he said he didn't understand. The officer told a marine to fire at us. The bullet whipped through the mizen. 'Bang' went one of the main-deck guns just over our heads. We felt a rush and shock, and our mizen mast and sail went over the side.

Marah stood up and raised his hand. 'We surrender, sir!' he shouted; 'we surrender! Down helm, boys.'

We swung round on our keel, and came to the wind. We saw the officer nod approval and speak a word to the sailing-master, and then the great ship lashed past us, a mighty, straining, heaving fabric of beauty, whose lower studding sails were wet half-way to their irons.

'Now for it!' said Marah. He hauled his wind, and the lugger shot off towards the broken water. 'If we get among those shoals,' he said, 'we're safe as houses. The frigate's done. She's going at such a pace they will never stop her. Not till she's gone a mile. Not without they rip the masts out of her. That officer ought to have known that trick. That will be a lesson to you, Mr Jim. If ever you're in a little ship, and you get chased by a big ship, you keep on till she's right on top of you, and then luff hard all you know, and the chances are you'll get a mile start before they come round to go after you.'

We had, in fact, doubled like a hare, and the frigate, like a greyhound, had torn on ahead, unable to turn. We saw her lower

THE FRIGATE 'LAOCOON' 131

stunsail boom carry away as they took in the sail, and we could see her seamen running to their quarters ready to brace the yards and bring the ship to her new course. The lugger soon gathered way and tore on, but it was now blowing very fresh indeed, and the sea before us was one lashing smother of breakers. Marah seemed to think nothing of that; he was watching the frigates. One, a slower sailer than the other, was sailing back to the fleet; the second had hove to about a mile away, with her longboat lowered to pursue us. The boat was just clear of her shadow; crowding all sail in order to get to us. The third ship, the ship which we had tricked, was hauling to the wind, with her light canvas clued up for furling. In a few moments she was braced up and standing towards us, but distant about a mile.

Suddenly both frigates opened fire, and the great cannon balls ripped up the sea all round us.

'They'll sink us, sure,' said one of the smugglers with a grin.

The men all laughed, and I laughed too; we were all so very much interested in what was going to happen. The guns fired steadily one after the other in a long rolling roar. The men laughed at each shot.

'They couldn't hit the sea,' they said derisively. 'The navy gunners are no use at all.'

'No,' said Marah, 'they're not. But if they keep their course another half-minute they'll be on the sunk reef, and a lot of 'em 'll be drowned. I wonder will the old *Laocoön* take a hint.'

'Give 'em the pennant,' said Gateo.

'Ay, give it 'em,' said half-a-dozen others. 'Don't let 'em wreck.'

Marah opened the flag-locker, and took out a blue pennant (it had a white ball in the middle of it), which he hoisted to his main truck. 'Let her go off,' he cried to the helmsman.

For just a moment we lay broadside on to the frigate, a fair target for her guns, so that she could see the pennant blowing out clear.

'You see, Jim?' asked Marah. 'That pennant means "You are standing in to danger." Now we will luff again.'

'I don't think they saw it, guv'nor,' said one of the sailors as another shot flew over us. 'They'll have to send below to get their glasses, those blind navy jokers.'

THE FRIGATE 'LAOCOON'

'Off,' said Marah, quickly; and again we lay broadside on, tumbling in the swell, shipping heavy sprays.

This time they saw it, for the *Laocoön's* helm was put down, her great sails shivered and threshed, and she stood off on the other tack. As she stood away we saw an officer leap on to the taffrail, holding on by the mizen backstays.

'Tar my wig,' said Marah, 'if he isn't bowing to us!'

Sure enough the officer took off his hat to us and bowed gracefully.

'Polite young man,' said Marah. 'We will give them the other pennant.'

Another flag, a red pennant, was hoisted in place of the blue. 'Wishing you a pleasant voyage,' said Marah. 'Now luff, my sons. That longboat will be on to us.'

Indeed, the longboat had crept to within six hundred yards of us; it was time we were moving, though the guns were no longer firing on us from the ships.

'Mind your helm, boys,' said Marah as he went forward to the bows. 'I've got to con you through a lot of bad rocks. You'll have to steer small or die.'

CHAPTER XII

BLACK POOL BAY

I SHALL not describe our passage through the Green Stones to Kermorvan, but in nightmares it comes back to me. We seemed to wander in blind avenues, hedged in by seas, and broken water, awful with the menace of death. For five or six hours we dodged among rocks and reefs, wet with the spray that broke upon them and sick at heart at the sight of the whirlpools and eddies. I think that they are called the Green Stones because the seas break over them in bright green heaps. Here and there among them the tide seized us and swept us along, and in the races where this happened there were sucking whirlpools, strong enough to twist us round. How often we were near our deaths I cannot think, but time and time again the backwash of a breaker came over our rail in a green mass. When

BLACK POOL BAY 135

we sailed into Kermorvan I was only half conscious from the cold and wet. I just remember some one helping me up some steps with seaweed on them.

We stayed in Kermorvan for a week or more, waiting for our cargo of brandy, silk, and tobacco, and for letters and papers addressed to the French war-prisoners in the huge prison on Dartmoor.

I was very unhappy in Kermorvan, thinking of home. It would have been less dismal had I had more to do, but I was unoccupied and a prisoner, in charge of an old French woman, who spoke little English, so that time passed slowly indeed. At last we set sail up the coast, hugging the French shore, touching at little ports for more cargo till we came to Cartaret. Here a French gentleman (he was a military spy) came aboard us, and then we waited two or three days for a fair wind. At last the wind drew to the east, and we spread all sail for home on a wild morning when the fishermen were unable to keep the sea.

At dusk we were so near to home that I could see the Start and the whole well-known coast from Salcombe to Dartmoor.

In fact I had plenty of time to see it, for we doused our sails several miles out to sea, and lay tossing in the storm to a sea-anchor, waiting for the short summer night to fall. When it grew dark enough (of course, in that time of year, it is never very dark even in a storm) we stole in, mile by mile, to somewhere off Flushing, where we showed a light. We showed it three times from the bow, and at the last showing a red light gleamed from Flushing Church. That was the signal to tell us that all was safe, so then we sailed into Black Pool Bay, where the breakers were beating fiercely in trampling ranks.

There were about a dozen men gathered together on the beach. We sailed right in, till we were within ten yards of the sands, and there we moored the lugger by the head and stern, so that her freight could be discharged. The men on the beach waded out through the surf (though it took them up to the armpits), and the men in the lugger passed the kegs and boxes to them. Waves which were unusually big would knock down the men in the water, burden and all, and then there would be laughter from all hands, and

BLACK POOL BAY 137

grumbles from the victim. I never saw men work harder. The freight was all flung out and landed and packed in half an hour. It passed out in a continual stream from both sides of the boat; everybody working like a person possessed. And when the lugger was nearly free of cargo, and the string of workers in the water was broken on the port side, it occurred to me that I had a chance of escape. It flashed into my mind that it was dark, that no one in the lugger was watching me, that the set of the tide would drive me ashore (I was not a good swimmer, but I knew that in five yards I should be able to touch bottom), and that in another two hours, or less, I should be in bed at home, with all my troubles at an end.

When I thought of escaping, I was standing alone at the stern. A lot of the boat's crew were in the water, going ashore to 'run' the cargo, on horseback, to the wilds of Dartmoor. The others were crowded at the bow, watching them go, or watching the men upon the beach, moving here and there by torchlight, packing the kegs on the horses' backs. It was a wild scene. The wind blew the torches into great red fiery banners; the waves hissed and spumed, and glimmered into brightness; you could see the horses shying, and the men hurrying to and fro; and now and then some one would cry out, and then a horse would whinny. All the time there was a good deal of unnecessary talk and babble; the voices and laughter of the seamen came in bursts as the wind lulled. Every now and then a wave would burst with a smashing noise, and the smugglers would laugh at those wetted by the spray. I saw that I had a better chance of landing unobserved on the port side; so I stole to that side, crawled over the gunwale, and slid into the sea without a splash.

The water made me gasp at first; but that only lasted a second. I made a gentle stroke or two towards the shore, trying not to raise my head much, and really I felt quite safe before I had made three strokes. When you swim in the sea at night, you see so little that you feel that you, in your turn, cannot be seen either. All that I could see was a confused mass of shore with torch-lights. Every now and then that would be hidden from me by the comb of a wave; and then a following wave would souse into my

BLACK POOL BAY

face and go clean over me; but as my one thought was to be hidden from the lugger, I rather welcomed a buffet of that sort. I very soon touched bottom, for the water near the beach is shallow. I stood up and bent over, so as not to be seen, and began to stumble towards the shelter of the rocks. The business of lading the horses was going steadily forward, with the same noisy hurry. I climbed out of the backwash of the last breaker, and dipped down behind a rock, high and dry on the sands. I was safe, I thought, safe at last, and I was too glad at heart to think of my sopping clothes, and of the cold which already made me shiver like an aspen. Suddenly, from up the hill, not more than a hundred yards from me, come the 'Hoo-hoo' of an owl, the smuggler's danger signal. The noise upon the beach ceased at once; the torches plunged into the sand and went out: I heard the lugger's crew cut their cables and hoist sail.

A voice said 'Carry on boys. The preventives are safe at Bolt Tail,' and at that the noise broke out as before.

Some one cried 'Sh,' and 'Still,' and in the silence which followed, the 'Hoo-hoo' of the owl called again, with a little flourishing note at the end of the call.

A man cried out, 'Mount and scatter.'

Some one else cried, 'Where's Marah?' and as I lay crouched, some one bent over me and touched me.

'Sorry, Jim,' said Marah's voice. 'I knew you'd try it. You only got your clothes wet. Come on, now.'

'Hoo-hoo' went the owl again, and at this, the third summons, we distinctly heard many horses' hooves coming at a gallop towards us, though at a considerable distance.

'Marah! Come on, man!' cried several voices.

'Come on,' said Marah, dragging me to the horses. 'Off, boys,' he called. 'Scatter as you ride.' Many horses moved off at a smart trot up the hill to Stoke Fleming. Their horses' feet were muffled with felt, so that they made little noise, although they were many.

Marah swung me up into the saddle of one of the three horses in his care. He himself rode the middle horse. I was on his off side. The horse I mounted had a keg of spirits lashed to the saddle behind

BLACK POOL BAY

me; the horse beyond Marah was laden like a pack-mule.

'We're the rearguard,' said Marah to me. 'We must bring them clear off. Ride boys —Strete road,' he called; and the smugglers of the rearguard clattered off by the back road, or broken disused lane, which leads to Allington. Still Marah waited, the only smuggler now left on the beach. The preventive officers were clattering down the hill to us, less than a quarter of a mile away. 'It's the preventives right enough,' he said, as a gust of wind brought the clatter of sabres to us, above the clatter of the hooves. 'We're in for a run to-night. Some one's been blabbing. I think I know who. Well, I pity him. That's what. I pity him. Here, boy. You ought not to ha' tried to cut. You'll be half frozen with the wet. Drink some of this.'

He handed me a flask, and forced me to take a gulp of something hot; it made me gasp, but it certainly warmed me, and gave me heart after my disappointment. I was too cold and too broken with misery to be frightened of the preventives. I only prayed that they might catch me and take me home.

We moved slowly to the meeting of the roads, and there Marah halted for a moment. Our horses stamped, and then whinnied. A horse on the road above us whinnied.

One of the clattering troop cried 'There they are. We have them. Come along, boys.'

Some one—I knew the voice—it was Captain Barmoor, of the Yeomanry—cried out 'Stand and surrender.' And then I saw the sabres gleam under the trees, and heard the horses' hooves grow furious upon the stones. Marah stood up in his stirrups, and put his fingers in his mouth, and whistled a long, wailing, shrill whistle. Then he kicked his horses and we started, at a rattling pace, up the wretched twisting lane which led to Allington.

Now, the preventives, coming downhill at a tearing gallop, could not take the sharp turn of the lane without pulling up; they got mixed in some confusion at the turning, and a horse and rider went into the ditch. We were up the steep rise, and stretching out at full tilt for safety, before they had cleared the corner. Our horses were fresh; theirs had trotted hard for some miles under heavy men, so that at the first sight the advantage lay with us; but their horses were better than ours, and in better trim for a gallop. Marah checked the three horses, and let them take it easy, till we turned into the well-remembered high road which leads from Strete to my home. Here, on the level, he urged them on, and the pursuit swept after us; and here in the open, I felt for the first time the excitement of the hunt. I wanted to be caught; I kept praying that my horse would come down, or that the preventives would catch us; and at the same time the hurry of our rush through the night set my blood leaping, made me cry aloud as we galloped, made me call to the horses to gallop faster. There was nothing on the road; no one was travelling; we had the highway to ourselves. Near the farm at the bend we saw men by the roadside, and an owl called to us from among them, with that little flourish at the end of the call which I had heard once before that evening. We dashed past them; but as Marah passed, he cried out, 'Yes. Be quick.' And behind us, as we sped along, we heard something dragged across the road. The crossways lay just beyond.

To my surprise, Marah never hesitated. He did not take the Allington road, but spurred uphill towards the 'Snail's Castle,' and the road to Kingsbridge. As we galloped, we heard a crash behind us, and the cry of a hurt horse, and the clatter of a sword upon the road. Then more cries sounded; we could hear our pursuers pulling up.

'They're into a tree-trunk,' said Marah. 'Some friends put a tree across, and one of them's gone into it. We shall probably lose them now,' he added. 'They will go on for Allington. Still, we mustn't wait yet.'

Indeed, the delay was only momentary. The noise of the horses soon re-commenced behind us; and though they paused at the cross-roads, it was only for a few seconds. Some of the troopers took the Allington road. Another party took the road which we had taken; and a third party stopped (I believe) to beat the farm buildings for the men who had laid the tree in the road.

We did not stop to see what they were doing, you may be sure; for when Marah saw that his trick had not shaken them off, he began to hurry his horses, and we were soon slipping and sliding down the steep zig-zag road which leads past 'Snail's Castle.' I had some half-formed notion of flinging

BLACK POOL BAY 145

myself off my horse as we passed the door, or of checking the horse I rode, and shouting for help. For there, beyond the corner, was the house where I had been so happy, and the light from the window lying in a yellow patch across the road; and there was Hoolie's bark to welcome us. Perhaps if I had not been wet and cold I might have made an attempt to get away; and I knew the preventives were too close to us for Marah to have lingered, had I done so.

But you must remember that we were riding very fast, that I was very young, and very much afraid of Marah, and that the cold and the fear of the preventives (for in a way I was horribly frightened by them) had numbed my brain.

'Don't you try it,' said Marah, grimly, as we came within sight of the house. 'Don't you try it.' He snatched my rein, bending forward on his horse's neck, calling a wild, queer cry. It was one of the gipsy horse-calls, and at the sound of it the horses seemed to lose their wits, for they dashed forward past the house, as though they were running away. It was as much as I could do to keep in the saddle. What made it so bitter to me was the opening of the window behind me. At the sound of the cry, and of those charging horses, some one—some one whom I knew so well, and loved so—ran to the window to look out. I heard the latch rattling and the jarring of the thrown-back sash, and I knew that some one—I would have given the world to have known who—looked out, and saw us as we swept round the corner and away downhill.

CHAPTER XIII

IN THE VALLEY

WE turned down the valley, along the coast-track, splashing through the little stream that makes it so boggy by the gate, and soon we were on the coach-road galloping along the straight two miles towards Tor Cross. Our horses were beginning to give way, for we had done four miles at good speed, and now the preventives began to gain upon us. Looking back as we galloped we could see them on the straight road, about two hundred yards away. Every time we looked back they seemed to be nearer, and at last Marah leant across and told me to keep low in my saddle, as he thought they were going to fire on us. A carbine shot cracked behind us, and I heard the 'zip' of the bullet over me.

A man ran out suddenly from one of the furze-bushes by the road, and a voice cried, 'Stop them, boys!' The road seemed suddenly full of people, who snatched at our reins, and hit us with sticks. I got a shrewd blow over the knee, and I heard Marah say something as he sent one man spinning to the ground. 'Crack, crack!' went the carbines behind us. Some one had hold of my horse's reins, shouting, 'I've got *you*, anyway!' Then Marah fired a pistol—it all happened in a second—the bullet missed, but the flash scorched my horse's nose; the horse reared, and knocked the man down, and then we were clear, and rattling along to Tor Cross.

Looking back, we saw one or two men getting up from the road, and then half-a-dozen guns and pistols flashed, and Marah's horse screamed and staggered. There was a quarter of a mile to go to Tor Cross, and that quarter-mile was done at such a speed as I have never seen since. Marah's horse took the bit in his teeth, and something of his terror was in our horses too.

In a moment, as it seemed, we were past the houses, and over the rocks by the brook-mouth; and there, with a groan, Marah's horse came down. Marah was evidently expecting it, for he had hold of my rein at the time, and as his horse fell he cleared the

IN THE VALLEY 149

body. 'Get down, Jim,' he said. 'We're done. The horses are cooked. They have had six miles; another mile would kill them. Poor beast's heart's burst. Down with you.' He lifted me off the saddle, and lashed the two living horses over the quarters with a strip of seaweed. He patted the dead horse, with a 'Poor boy,' and dragged me down behind one of the black rocks, which crop up there above the shingle.

The two horses bolted off along the strand, scattering the pebbles, and then, while the clash of their hooves was still loud upon the stones, the preventives came pounding up, their horses all badly blown and much distressed. Their leader was Captain Barmoor. I knew him by his voice.

'Here's a dead horse!' he cried. 'Sergeant, we have one of their horses. Get down and see if there's any contraband upon him. After them, you others. We shall get them now. Ride on, I tell you! What are you pulling up for?'

The other preventives crashed on over the shingle. Captain Barmoor and the sergeant remained by the dead horse. Marah and I lay close under the rock, hardly daring to breathe, and wondering very much whether we made any visible mark to the tall man on his horse. Shots rang out from the preventives' carbines, and the gallopers made a great dash upon the stones. We heard the sergeant's saddle creak, only a few yards away, and then his boots crunched on the beach as he walked up to the dead horse.

'No. There be no tubs here, sir,' he said, after a short examination. 'Her be dead enough. Stone dead, sir. There's an empty pistol-case, master.'

'Oh,' said Captain Barmoor. 'Any saddle-bag, or anything of that kind?'

The man fumbled about in the gear, 'No, there was nothing of that kind—nothing at all.'

'Bring on the saddle,' said the captain. 'There may be papers stitched in it.' We heard the sergeant unbuckling the girth. 'By the way,' said the captain, 'you're sure the third horse was led?'

'Yes,' said the sergeant. 'Two and a led horse there was, sir.'

'H'm,' said the captain. 'I wonder if they have dismounted. They might have. Look about among the rocks there.'

IN THE VALLEY 151

I saw Marah's right hand raise his horse-pistol, as the sergeant stepped nearer. In another moment he must have seen us. If he had even looked down, he could not have failed to see us: but he stood within six feet of us, looking all round him—looking anywhere but at his feet. Then he walked away from us, and looked at the rocks near the brook.

'D'ye see them?' snapped the captain.

'No, sir. Nothin' of 'em. They ben't about here, sir. I think they've ridden on. Shall I look in the furze there, sir, afore we go?'

'No,' said the captain. 'Well, yes. Just take a squint through it.'

But as the sergeant waddled uneasily in his sea-boots across the shingle, the carbines of the preventives cracked out in a volley about a quarter of a mile away. A shot or two followed the volley.

'A shot-gun that last, sir,' said the sergeant.

'Yes,' said the captain. 'Come along. There's another. Come, mount, man. They're engaged.'

We heard the sergeant's horse squirming about as the sergeant tried to mount, and then the two galloped off. Voices sounded close beside us, and feet moved upon the sand. 'Still!' growled Marah in my ear. Some one cried out 'Further on. They're fighting further on. Hurry up and we shall see it.'

About a dozen Tor Cross men were hurrying up, in the chance of seeing a skirmish. The wife of one of them—old Mrs Rivers—followed after them, calling to her man to come back. 'I'll give it to 'ee, if 'ee don't come back. Come back, I tell 'ee.' They passed on rapidly, pursued by the angry woman, while more shots banged and cracked further and further along the shore.

We waited till they passed out of hearing, and then Marah got up. 'Come on, son,' he said. 'We must be going. Lucky your teeth didn't chatter, or they'd have heard us.'

'I wish they had heard us.' I cried, hotly. 'Then I'd have gone home to-night. Let me go, Marah. Let me go home.'

'Next trip, Jim,' he said kindly. 'Not this. I want you to learn about life. You will get mewed up with them ladies else, and then you will never do anything.'

IN THE VALLEY

'Ah,' I said. 'But if you don't let me go I'll scream. Now then. I'll scream.'

'Scream away, son,' said Marah, calmly. 'There's not many to hear you. But you'll not get home after what you have seen to-night. Come on, now.'

He took me by the collar, and walked me swiftly to a little cove, where one or two of the Tor Cross fishers kept their boats. I heard a gun or two away in the distance, and then a great clatter of shingle, as the coastguards' horses trotted back towards us, with the led horse between two of them, as the prize of the night. They did not hear us, and could not see us, and Marah took good care not to let me cry out to them. He just turned my face up to his, and muttered, 'You just try it. You try it, son, and I'll hold you in the sea till you choke.'

The wind was blowing from the direction of the coastguards towards us, and even if I had cried out, perhaps, they would never have heard me. You may think me a great coward to have given in in this way; but few boys of my age would have made much outcry against a man like Marah. He made the heart die within you; and to me, cold and wet from my ducking, terrified of capture in spite of my innocence (for I was not at all sure that the smugglers would not swear that I had joined them, and had helped them in their fights and escapades), the outlook seemed so hopeless and full of misery that I could do nothing. My one little moment of mutiny was gone, my one little opportunity was lost. Had I made a dash for it—— But it is useless to think in that way.

Marah got into the one boat which floated in the little artificial creek, and thrust me down into the stern sheets. Then he shoved her off with a stretcher (the oars had been carried to the fisher's house, there were none in the boat), and as soon as we were clear of the rocks, in the rather choppy sea, he stepped the stretcher in the mast-crutch as a mast, and hoisted his coat as a sail. He made rough sheets by tying a few yards of spun-yarn to the coat-skirts, and then, shipping the rudder, he bore away before the wind towards the cave by Black Pool.

We had not gone far (certainly not fifty yards), when we saw the horses of the coast-guards galloping down to the sea, one of the

IN THE VALLEY 155

horses shying at the whiteness of the breaking water.

A voice hailed us. 'Boat ahoy!' it shouted; 'what are you doing in the boat there?'

And then all the horsemen drew up in a clump among the rocks.

'Us be drifting, master,' shouted Marah, speaking in the broad dialect of the Devon men; 'us be drifting.'

'Come in till I have a look at you,' cried the voice again. 'Row in to the rocks here.'

'Us a-got no o-ars,' shouted Marah, letting the boat slip on. 'Lie down, son,' he said; 'they will fire in another minute.'

Indeed, we heard the ramrods in the carbines and the loud click of the gun-cocks.

'Boat ahoy!' cried the voice again. 'Row in at once! D'ye hear? Row in at once, or I shall fire on you.'

Marah did not answer.

'Present arms!' cried the voice again after a pause; and at that Marah bowed down in the stern sheets under the gunwale.

'Fire!' said the voice; and a volley ripped up the sea all round us, knocking off splinters from the planks and flattening out against the transom.

'Keep down, Jim; you're all right,' said Marah. 'We will be out of range in another minute.'

Bang! came a second volley, and then single guns cracked and banged at intervals as we drew away.

For the next half-hour we were just within extreme range of the carbines and musketoons. During that half-hour we were slowly slipping by the long two miles of Slapton sands. We could not go fast, for our only sail was a coat, and, though the wind was pretty fresh, the set of the tide was against us. So for half an hour we crouched below that rowboat's gunwale, just peeping up now and then to see the white line of the breakers on the sand, and beyond that the black outlines of the horsemen, who slowly followed us, firing steadily, but with no very clear view of what they fired at. I thought that the two miles would never end. Sometimes the guns would stop for a minute, and I would think, 'Ah! now we are out of range,' or, 'Now they have given us up.' And then, in another second, another volley would rattle at us, and perhaps a bullet would go whining overhead, or a heavy chewed slug would come 'pob' into the boat's side within six inches of me.

Marah didn't seem to mind their firing. He was too pleased at having led the preventives away from the main body of the night-riders to mind a few bullets. 'Ah, Jim,' he said, 'there's three thousand pounds in lace, brandy, and tobacco gone to Dartmoor this night. And all them red-coat fellers got was a dead horse and a horse with a water-breaker on him. And the dead horse was their own, *and* the one they took. I stole 'em out of the barrack stables myself.'

'But horse-stealing is a capital offence,' I cried. 'They could hang you.'

'Yes,' he said; 'so they would if they could.' Bang! came another volley of bullets all round us. 'They'd shoot us, too, if they could, so far as that goes; but so far, they haven't been able. Never cross any rivers till you come to the water, Jim. Let that be a lesson to you.'

I have often thought of it since as sound advice, and I have always tried to act upon it; but at the time it didn't give much comfort.

At the end of half an hour we were clear of Slapton sands, and coming near to Strete, and here even Marah began to be uneasy.

He was watching the horsemen on the beach very narrowly, for as soon as they had passed the Lea they had stopped firing on us, and had gone at a gallop to the beach boathouse to get out a boat.

'What are they doing, Marah?' I asked.

'Getting out a boat to come after us,' he answered. 'Silly fools! If they'd done that at once they'd have got us. They may do it now. There goes the boat.'

We heard the cries of the men as the boat ground over the shingle. Then we heard shouts and cries, and saw a light in the boathouse.

'Looking for oars and sails,' said Marah, 'and there are none. Good, there are none.'

Happily for us, there were none. But we heard a couple of horses go clattering up the road to O'Farrell's cottage to get them.

'We shall get away now,' said Marah.

In a few minutes we were out of sight of the beach. Then one of the strange coast currents caught us, and swept us along finely for a few minutes. Soon our boat was in the cave, snugly lashed to the ring-bolts, and Marah had lifted me up the stairs to the room where a few smugglers lay in their hammocks, sleeping heavily. Marah made me drink something and eat some pigeon pie; and then, stripping my clothes from me, he rubbed me down with a blanket, wrapped me in a pile of blankets, and laid me to sleep in a corner on an old sail.

CHAPTER XIV

A TRAITOR

THE next day, when I woke, a number of smugglers had come back from their ride. They were sitting about the cave, in their muddy clothes, in high good spirits. They had been chased by a few preventives as far as Allington, and there they had had a brisk skirmish with the Allington police, roused by the preventives' carbine fire. They had beaten off their opponents, and had reached Dartmoor in safety.

'Yes,' said Marah; 'all very well. But we have been blabbed on. We had the cutter on us on our way out, and here we were surprised coming home. It was the Salcombe cutter chased us, and it was the Salcombe boys gave the preventives the tip last night. Otherwise they'd have been in Salcombe all last night, watching Bolt Tail, no less. 'Stead of that, they came lumbering here, and jolly near nabbed us. Now, it's

A TRAITOR

one of us. There's no one outside knows anything: and only half-a-dozen in Salcombe knew our plans. Salcombe district supplies North Devon; we supply to the east more. Who could it be, boys?'

Some said one thing, some another. And then a man suggested 'the parson'; and when he said that it flashed across my mind that he meant Mr Cottier, for I knew that sailors always called a schoolmaster a parson, and I remembered how Mrs Cottier had heard his voice among the night-riders on the night of the snow-storm just before Christmas.

'No; it couldn't be the parson,' said some one. 'No one trusts the parson.'

'I don't know as it couldn't be,' said the man whom they called Hankie. 'He is a proper cunning one to pry out.'

'Ah!' said another smuggler. 'And, come to think of it, we passed him the afternoon afore we sailed. I was driving with the Captain. I was driving the Captain here from Kingsbridge.'

'He knows the Captain,' said Marah grimly. 'He might have guessed—seeing him with you—that you were coming to arrange a run. Now, how would he know where we were bound?'

'Guessed it,' said Hankie. 'He's been on a run or two with the Salcombe fellers. Besides, he couldn't be far out.'

'No,' said Marah, musingly; 'he couldn't. And a hint would have been enough to send the cutter after us.'

'But how did he put them on us last night?' said another smuggler. 'We had drawn them out proper to Bolt Tail to look for a cargo there. Properly we had drawed them. Us had a boat and all, showing lights.'

'Well, if it was the parson who done it, he'd easily find a way,' said Marah. 'We had better go over and see about it.'

Before they went they left me in charge of the old Italian man, who taught me how to point a rope, which is one of the prettiest kinds of plaiting ever invented. The day passed slowly—oh! so slowly; for a day like that, so near home, yet so far away, and with so much misery in prospect, was agonising. I wondered what they would do to Mr Cottier; I wondered if ever I should get home again; I wondered whether the coastguards would have sufficient sense to arrest Marah if they saw him on the roads. In wondering like this, the day slowly dragged to an end; and at the end of the day, just before a watery sunset, Marah and the others returned, leading Mr Cottier as their prisoner.

It shows you what power the night-riders had in those days. They had gone to Salcombe to Mr Cottier's lodgings; they had questioned him, perhaps with threats, till he had confessed that he had betrayed them to the preventives; then they had gagged him, hustled him downstairs to a waiting closed carriage, and then they had quietly driven him on, undisturbed, to their fastness in the cliff. It was sad to see a man fallen so low, a man who had been at the University, and master of a school. It was sad to see him, his flabby face all fallen in and white from excess of fear, and to see his eyes lolling about from one to another man, trying to find a little hope in the look of the faces in the fast-darkening cave.

'Well,' he said surlily at last; 'you have got me. What are you going to do to me?'

'What d'ye think you deserve?' said Marah. 'Eh? You'd have had us all hanged and glad, too. You'll see soon enough what we're going to do to you.' He struck a light for his pipe, and lit a candle in a corner of the cave near where I lay. 'You'll soon know *your* fate,' he added. 'Meanwhile, here's a friend of yours—one you might like to talk to. You'll not get another chance.'

At this the man grovelled on the cave floor, crying out to them to let him live, that he would give them all his money, and so on.

'Get up,' said Marah; 'get up. Try and act like a man, even if you aren't one.'

The man went on wailing, 'What are you going to do to me?—what are you going to do to me?'

'Spike your guns,' said Marah, curtly. 'There's your friend in the corner. Talk to him.'

He left us together in the cave; an armed smuggler sat at the cave entrance, turning his quid meditatively.

'Mr Cottier,' I said, 'do you remember Jim—Jim Davis?'

'Jim!' cried Mr Cottier; 'Jim, how did you come here?'

'By accident,' I said; 'and now I'm a prisoner here, like you.'

A TRAITOR   165

'Oh, Jim,' he cried, 'what are they going to do to me? You must have heard them. What are they going to do to me? Will they kill me, Jim?'

I thought of the two coastguards snugly shut up in France, in one of the inns near Brest, living at free-quarters, till the smugglers thought they could be sure of them. When I thought of those two men I felt that the traitor would not be killed; and yet I was not sure. I believe they would have killed him if I had not been there. They were a very rough lot, living rough lives, and a traitor put them all in peril of the gallows. Smugglers were not merciful to traitors (it is said that they once tied a traitor to a post at low-water mark, and let the tide drown him), and Marah's words made me feel that Mr Cottier would suffer some punishment: not death, perhaps, but something terrible.

I tried to reassure the man, but I could say very little. And I was angry with him, for he never asked after his wife, nor after Hugh, his son: and he asked me nothing of my prospects. The thought of his possible death by violence within the next few hours kept him from all thought of other people. Do not blame him. We who have not been tried do not know how we should behave in similar circumstances.

By-and-by the men came back to us. We were led downstairs, and put aboard the lugger. Then the boat pushed off silently, sail was hoisted, and a course was set down channel, under a press of canvas. Mr Cottier cheered up when we had passed out of the sight of the lights of the shore, for he knew then that his life was to be spared. His natural bullying vein came back to him. He sang and joked, and even threatened his captors. So all that night we sailed, and all the next day and night—a wild two or three days' sailing, with spray flying over us, and no really dry or warm place to sleep in, save a little half-deck which they rigged in the bows.

I should have been very miserable had not Marah made me work with the men, hauling the ropes, swabbing down the decks, scrubbing the paintwork, and even bearing a hand at the tiller. The work kept me from thinking. The watches (four hours on, four hours off), which I had to keep like the other men, made the time pass rapidly; for

A TRAITOR

the days slid into each other, and the nights, broken into as they were by the night-watches, seemed all too short for a sleepy head like mine.

Towards the end of the passage, when the weather had grown brighter and hotter, I began to wonder how much further we were going. Then, one morning, I woke up to find the lugger at anchor in one of the ports of Northern Spain, with dawn just breaking over the olive-trees, and one or two large, queer-looking, lateen-rigged boats, xebecs from Africa, lying close to us. One of them was flying a red flag, and I noticed that our own boat was alongside of her. I thought nothing of it, but drew a little water from the scuttle-butt, and washed my face and hands in one of the buckets. One or two of the men were talking at my side.

'Ah!' said one of them, 'that's nine he did that way—nine, counting him.'

'A good job, too,' said another man. 'It's us or them. I'd rather it was them.'

'Yes,' said another fellow; 'and I guess they repent.'

The others laughed a harsh laugh, turning to the African boat with curious faces, to watch our boat pulling back, with Marah at her steering oar.

I noticed, at breakfast (which we all ate together on the deck), that Mr Cottier was no longer aboard the lugger. I had some queer misgivings, but said nothing till afterwards, when I found Marah alone.

'Marah,' I said, 'where is Mr Cottier? What have you done to him?'

He grinned at me grimly, as though he were going to refuse to tell me. Then he beckoned me to the side of the boat. 'Here,' he said, pointing to the lateen-rigged xebec; 'you see that felucca-boat?'

'Yes,' I said.

'Well, then,' Marah continued, 'he's aboard her—down in her hold: tied somewhere on the ballast. That's where Mr Cottier is. Now you want to know what we have done to him? Hey? Well, we've enlisted him in the Spanish Navy. That felucca-boat is what they call a tender. They carry recruits to the Navy in them boats. He will be in a Spanish man-of-war by this time next week. They give him twenty dollars to buy a uniform. He's about ripe for the Spanish Navy.'

A TRAITOR 169

'But, Marah,' I cried, 'he may have to fight against our ships.'

'All the better for us,' he answered. 'I wish all our enemies were as easy jobs.'

I could not answer for a moment; then I asked if he would ever get free again.

'I could get free again,' said Marah; 'but that man isn't like me. He's enlisted for three years. I doubt the war will last so long. The free trade will be done by the time he's discharged. You see, Jim, we free-traders can only make a little while the nations are fighting. By this time three years Mr Cottier can talk all he's a mind.'

I had never liked Mr Cottier, but I felt a sort of pity for him. Then I felt that perhaps the discipline would be the making of him, and that, if he kept steady, he might even rise in the Spanish Navy, since he was a man of education. Then I thought of poor Mrs Cottier at home, and I felt that her husband must be saved at all costs.

'Oh, Marah,' I cried, 'don't let him go like that. Go and buy him back. He doesn't deserve to end like that.'

'Rot!' said Marah, turning on his heel.

'Hands up anchor! Forward to the windlass, Jim. You know your duty.'

The men ran to their places. Very soon we were under sail again, out at sea, with the Spanish coast in the distance astern, a line of bluish hills, almost like clouds.

CHAPTER XV

THE BATTLE ON THE SHORE

WE had rough weather on the passage north, so that we were forced to go slowly creeping from port to port, from Bayonne to Fécamp, always in dread of boats of the English frigates, which patrolled the whole coast, keeping the French merchantmen shut up in harbour.

As we stole slowly to the north, I thought of nothing but the new Spanish sailor. He would be living on crusts, so the smugglers told me; and always he would have an overseer to prod him with a knife if, in a moment of sickness or weariness, he faltered in his work, no matter how hard it might be. But by this time I had learned that the smugglers loved to frighten me. I know now that there was not a word of truth in any of the tales they told me.

At Etaples we were delayed for nearly a

fortnight, waiting, first of all, for cargo, and then a fair wind. There were two other smugglers' luggers at Etaples with us. They were both waiting for the wind to draw to the south or south-east, so that they could dash across to Romney Sands.

As they had more cargo than they could stow, they induced Marah to help them by carrying their surplus. They were a whole day arguing about it before they came to terms; but it ended, as we all knew that it would end, by Marah giving the other captains drink, and leading them thus to him whatever terms they asked.

The other smugglers in our boat were not very eager to work with strangers; but Marah talked them over. Only old Gateo would not listen to him.

'Something bad will come of it,' he kept saying. 'You mark what I say: something bad will come of it.'

Then Marah would heave a sea-boot at him, and tell him to hold his jaw; and the old man would mutter over his quid and say that we should see.

We loaded our lugger with contraband goods, mostly lace and brandy, an extremely

THE BATTLE ON THE SHORE 173

valuable cargo. The work of loading kept the men from thinking about Gateo's warnings, though, like most sailors, they were all very superstitious. Then some French merchants gave us a dinner at the inn, to wish us a good voyage, and to put new spirit into us, by telling us what good fellows we were. But the dinner was never finished; for before they had begun their speeches a smuggler came in to say that the wind had shifted, and that it was now breezing up from the south-east. So we left our plates just as they were. The men rose up from their chairs, drank whatever was in their cups at the moment, and marched out of the inn in a body.

To me it seemed bitterly cold outside the inn. I shivered till my teeth chattered.

Marah asked me if I had a touch of fever, or if I were ill, or 'what was it, anyway, that made me shiver so?'

I said that I was cold.

'Cold!' he said. 'Cold? Why, it's one of the hottest nights we have had this summer. Here's a youngster says he's cold!'

One or two of them laughed at me then; for it was, indeed, a hot night. They laughed and chaffed together as they cast off the mooring ropes.

For my part, I felt that my sudden chilly fit was a warning that there was trouble coming. I can't say why I felt that, but I felt it; and I believe that Marah in some way felt it, too. Almost the last thing I saw that night, as I made up my bed under the half-deck among a few sacks and bolts of canvas, was Marah scowling and muttering, as though uneasy, at the foot of the foremast, from which he watched the other luggers as they worked out of the river ahead of us.

'He, too, feels uneasy,' I said to myself.

Then I fell into a troubled doze, full of dreams of sea-monsters, which flapped and screamed at me from the foam of the breaking seas.

I was not called for a watch that night. In the early morning, between one and two o'clock, I was awakened by a feeling that something was about to happen. I sat up, and then crept out on to the deck, and there, sure enough, something was about to happen. Our sails were down, we were hardly moving through the water, the water gurgled and plowtered under our keel, there was a light

THE BATTLE ON THE SHORE 175

mist fast fading before the wind. It was not very dark, in fact it was almost twilight. One or two stars were shining; there were clouds slowly moving over them; but the sky astern of us was grey and faint yellow, and the land, the Kentish coast, lay clear before us, with the nose of Dungeness away on our port bow. It was all very still and beautiful. The seamen moved to and fro about the lugger. Dew dipped from our rigging; the decks were wet with dew, the drops pattered down whenever the lugger rolled. The other boats lay near us, both of them to starboard. Their sails were doused in masses under the mast. I could see men moving about; I could hear the creaking of the blocks, as the light roll drew a rope over a sheave.

The boats were not very close to the shore; but it was so still, so very peaceful, that we could hear the waves breaking on the beach with a noise of hushing and of slipping shingle, as each wave passed with a hiss to slither back in a rush of foam broken by tiny stones. A man in the bows of the middle lugger showed a red lantern, and then doused it below the half-deck. He showed it three times; and at the third showing, we all turned to the shore, to see what signal the red light would bring. The shore was open before us. In the rapidly growing light, we could make out a good deal of the lie of the land. From the northern end of the beach an answering red light flashed; and then, nearer to us, a dark body was seen for a moment, kindling two green fires at a little distance from each other. Our men were not given to nervousness, they were rough, tough sailors; but they were all relieved when our signals were answered.

'It's them,' they said. 'It's all right. Up with the foresail. We must get the stuff ashore. It'll be dawn in a few minutes, and then we shall have the country on us.'

'Heave ahead, boys!' cried one of the men in the next lugger as she drove past us to the shore.

'Ay! Heave ahead,' said Marah, eyeing the coast.

He took the tiller as the lugger gathered way under her hoisted foresail. While we slipped nearer to the white line of the breakers along the sand. he muttered under his breath

THE BATTLE ON THE SHORE 177

(I was standing just beside him) in a way which frightened me.

'I dunno,' he said aloud. 'But I've a feeling that there's going to be trouble. I never liked this job. Here it is, almost daylight, and not an ounce of stuff ashore. I'd never have come this trip if the freights hadn't been so good. Here, you,' he cried suddenly to one of the men. 'Don't you pass the gaskets. You'll furl no sails till you're home, my son. Pass the halliards along so that you can hoist in a jiffy.' Then he hailed the other luggers. 'Ahoy there!' he called. 'You mind your eyes for trouble.'

His words caused some laughter in the other boats. In our boat, they caused the men to look around at Marah almost anxiously. He laughed and told them to stand by. Then we saw that the beach was crowded with men and horses, as at Black Pool, a week or two before. In the shallow water near the beach, we dropped our killick. The men from the beach waded out to us, our own men slipped over the side. The tubs and bales began to pass along the lines of men, to the men in charge of the horses. Only one word was spoken;

the word 'Hurry.' At every moment, as it seemed to me (full as I was of anxiety), the land showed more clearly, the trees stood out more sharply against the sky, the light in the east became more like a flame.

'Hurry,' said Marah. 'It'll be dawn in a tick.'

Hurry was the watchword of the crews. The men worked with a will. Tub after tub was passed along. Now and then we heard a splash and an oath. Then a horse would whinny upon the beach, startled by a wave, and a man would tell him to 'Stand back,' or 'Woa yer.' I caught the excitement, and handed out the tubs with the best of them.

I suppose that we worked in this way for half an hour or a little more. The men had worked well at Black Pool, where the run had been timed to end in darkness. Now that they had to race the daylight they worked like slaves under an overseer. One string of horses trotted off, fully loaded. within twenty minutes. A second string was led down; in the growing light I could see them stamping and tossing; they were backed right down into the sea, so that the water washed upon their hocks.

THE BATTLE ON THE SHORE 179

'Here, Jim,' said Marah suddenly, stopping me in my work, 'come here to me. Look here,' he said, when I stood before him. 'It's getting too light for this game. We may have to cut and run. Take this hatchet here, and go forward to the bows. When I say "cut," you cut, without looking round. Cut the cable, see? Cut it in two, mucho pronto. And you, Hankin—you, Gateo. Stand by the halliards, stretch them along ready to hoist. No. Hoist them. Don't wait. Hoist them now.'

One or two others lent their hands at the halliards, and the sails were hoisted. The men in the other luggers laughed and jeered.

'What are you hoisting sail for?' they cried.

'Sail-drill of a forenoon,' cried another, perhaps a deserter from the navy.

'Shut up,' Marah answered. 'Don't mind them, boys. Heave round. Heave round at what you're doing. Over with them tubs, sons! My hat! Those fellows are mad to be playing this game in a light like this. There's a fort within three miles of us.'

He had hardly finished speaking, when one of the men at the side of the lugger suddenly looked towards the beach, as though he had caught sight of something.

'Something's up,' he said sharply.

The beach and the shore beyond were both very flat in that part; nothing but marshy land, overgrown with tussock grass, and a few sand-dunes, covered with bents. It was not a country which could give much cover to an enemy; but in that half-light one could not distinguish very clearly, and an enemy could therefore take risks impossible in full day.

'A lot of cattle there,' said the smuggler who had spoken. 'It's odd there being so many.'

'Don't you graze many cattle here?' said Marah, looking ashore.

'What! in the marsh?' said the man. 'Not much.'

'Them's no cattle,' said Marah, after a pause. 'Them's not cows. Them's horses. Sure they're horses. Yes, and there's men mounting them. They have crawled up, leading their horses, and now we're done. Look out boys!' he shouted. 'Look out! Get on board.'

Even as he spoke the whole shore seemed to bristle with cavalry. Each slowly moving

THE BATTLE ON THE SHORE 181

horse stopped a moment, for his rider to mount. There were fifty or sixty of them: they seemed to spread all along the edge of the bay except at the northern end, where the line was not quite closed.

'Sentries asleep,' said Marah. 'This is the way they carry on in Kent. Yes. There's the sentry. Asleep on the sand-dune. Oh, yes. Time to wake up it is. You Mahon ape. Look at him.'

We saw the sentry leap to his feet, almost under the nose of a horse. He was too much surprised even to fire his pistol. He just jumped up, all dazed, holding up his hands to show that he surrendered. We saw two men on foot secure his hands. That was our first loss.

It all happened very, very quickly. We were taken by surprise, all unready, with our men ashore or mixed among the horses, or carrying tubs in the water. The troops and preventives were over the last dune and galloping down the sand to us almost before Marah had finished speaking; yet even then in all the confusion, as a captain shouted to us to 'surrender in the name of the King,' the smugglers were not without resource. A young man in a blue Scotch bonnet jumped on one of the horses, snatching another horse by the rein; half-a-dozen others did the same; the second string, half-loaded, started as they were up the sand and away at full gallop for the north end of the bay, where no soldiers showed as yet.

It was done in an instant of time; drilled horsemen could not have done it; the little man in the blue bonnet saw the one loophole and dashed for it. There was no shouting. One or two men spoke, and then there it was—done. Practically all the horses were lashing along the beach, going full tilt for safety: they galloped in a body like a troop of cavalry. Two preventives rode at them to stop them, but they rode slap into the preventives, tumbled them over, horse and man and then galloped on, not looking back. A trooper reined in, whipped up his carbine and fired, and that was the beginning of the fight. Then there came a general volley; pistols and carbines cracked and banged; a lot of smoke blew about the beach and along the water; our men shouted to each other; the soldiers cheered.

In another ten seconds a battle was going

THE BATTLE ON THE SHORE

on in the water all round us. The horsemen urged their horses right up to the sides of the luggers. The men in the water hacked at the horses' legs with their hangers; the horses screamed and bit. I saw one wounded horse seize a smuggler by the arm and shake him as a dog shakes a rat; the rider of the horse, firing at the man, shot the horse by accident through the head. I suppose he was too much excited to know what he was doing—I fancy that men in a battle are never quite sane. The horse fell over in the water, knocking down another horse, and then there was a lashing in the sea as the horse tried to rise. The smugglers cut at him in the sea, and all the time his rider was half under water trying to get up and pulling at the trigger of his useless, wetted pistol.

It all happened so quickly, that was the strange thing. In one minute we were hard at work at the tubs, in the next we were struggling and splashing, hacking at each other with swords, firing in each other's faces. Half-a-dozen horsemen tried to drag the lugger towards the shore, but the men beat them back. knocked them from their saddles, or flogged the horses over the nose with pistol-butts.

All this time the guns were banging, men were crying out, horses were screaming; it was the most confused thing I ever saw.

Marah knocked down a trooper with a broken cleat and shouted to me to cut the cable—which I did at once. One or two men ran to trim sail, and Marah took the tiller. At that moment a trooper rode into the sea just astern of us—I remember to this day the brightness of the splash his horse made; Marah turned at the noise and shot the horse; but the man fired too, and Marah seemed to stagger and droop over the tiller as though badly hit. Seeing that, I ran aft to help him. It seemed to me as I ran that the side of the lugger was all red with clambering, shouting soldiers, all of them firing pistols at me.

Marah picked himself up as I got there. 'Out of the way boy,' he cried. Two or three smugglers rallied round him. There were more shots, more cries. Half-a-dozen redcoats came aft in a rush; someone hit me a blow on the head, and all my life seemed to pass from me in a stream of fire out at my eyes. The last thing which I remember of the tussle was the face of the man who hit me. He was a pale man with wide eyes, his helmet knocked off, his stock loose at his throat; I just saw him as I fell, and then everything passed from my sight in a sound of roaring, like the roaring of waters in spate.

CHAPTER XVI

DRIFTING

When I recovered consciousness, the sun had risen; it was bright daylight all about us. That was really the first thing which I saw—the light of the sun on the deck. I struggled up to a sitting position, feeling great pain in my head. Marah lying over the tiller was the next thing which I saw; he was dead, I thought. Then I realised what had happened; we had had a fight. We were not under control; we were drifting with the tide up and down, with our sails backing and filling; up and down the deck there were wounded men, some of them preventives, some of them smugglers—poor Hankin was one of them. When I stood up I saw that I was the only person on his feet in the boat: it was not strange, perhaps.

Some of our men had gone with the horses, others had been in the water when the horse-

DRIFTING 187

men first charged them; probably all of those who had been in the water were either killed or taken. We had had four men aboard during the attack: of these one was badly hurt, another (Marah) was unconscious, the remaining two were drinking under the half-deck, having opened a tub of spirits. When I had stood up I felt a little stronger; I heard Marah moan a little. I tottered to the scuttle-butt, where we kept our drinking water; I splashed the contents of a couple of pannikins over my head and then drank about a pint and a half; that made me feel a different being. I was then able to do something for the others.

First of all I managed to help Marah down from his perch over the tiller: he had fallen across it with his head and hands almost touching the deck. I helped him, or rather, lifted him—for he could not help himself —to the deck; it was as much as I could do, he was so big and heavy. I put a tub under his head as a pillow, then I cut his shirt open and saw that he had been shot in the chest. I ran forward with a pannikin, drew some water, and gave him a drink. He drank greedily, biting the tin, but did not recognise me; all that he could say was 'Rip-raps, Rip-raps,' over and over again. The Rip-raps was the name of a race or tideway on the Campeachy coast; he had often told me about it, and I had remembered the name because it was such a queer one. I bathed his wound with the water.

After I had done what I could for Marah, I did the same for the wounded soldier. He thanked me for my trouble in a little, low, weak voice, infinitely serious—he seemed to think that I didn't believe him. 'I say, thank you, thank you,' he repeated earnestly, and then he gave a little gasp and fainted away in the middle of his thanks.

At that, I stood up and began to cry. I had had enough of misery, and that was more than I could bear. Between my sobs I saw—I did not observe, I just saw—that the lugger was drifting slowly northward, clear of Little Stone Point, as the smugglers had called it. I didn't much care where we drifted, but having seen so much, it occurred to me to see where the other luggers were.

One of them, I saw, was on her course for France, a couple of miles away already; the other was going for Dungeness, no doubt to pick up more hands somewhere on the Dunge Marsh. It was like them, I thought, to go off like that, leaving us to have the worst of the fight and every chance of being taken; they only thought of their own necks. When I saw that they had deserted us without even pausing to put a helmsman aboard us, I knew that there was no honour among thieves. There is not, in spite of what the proverb says. We were left alone—a boy, two drunkards, and some wounded men, within half a mile of the shore.

I looked for the preventives, but I could not see them. Most of them had gone after the horses across Romney Marsh. I did not know till long afterwards that the smugglers had beaten off the rest of the party, killing some and about twenty horses, and wounding nearly every other man engaged. It had been, in fact, a very determined battle, one of the worst ever fought between the smugglers and the authorities on that coast. As soon as the fight was over, the luggers got out from the shore, and the troops made off with their wounded to report at the fort, and to signal the Ness cutter to go in chase. At the moment when I looked for them they must, I think, have been rallying again. I could not see them, that was enough for me. Years afterwards I talked with one of the survivors, an old cavalry-man. He told me how the fight had seemed to him as he rode in at us.

'And d'ye know, sir,' he said, 'they had a boy forward ready with an axe to cut the cable, so I fired at him' ('Thank you,' I thought); 'and just as I pulled the trigger one of their men hit my gee a welt, and down he came in the water, and so, of course, I missed. But for that, sir, we'd have got them.'

I wondered which of the men had saved my life by hitting that 'gee a welt.' I wondered if he had been killed or taken, or whether he had got aboard us afterwards, or whether one of the other luggers had saved him. Well, I shall never know on this side of the grave. But it is odd is it not, that one should have one's life saved and never know that it was in danger till twenty years afterwards, when the man who saved it was never likely to be found? But I am getting away from my story.

I soon saw that the current was slowly

DRIFTING

setting us ashore. Marah, with his great manliness, had steered the lugger out to sea for some six hundred yards before he had collapsed. Then his fellows, seeing him, as they supposed, dead, turned to drinking. The lugger, left to herself, took charge, and swung round head to wind. Since then she had drifted, sometimes making a stern-board, sometimes going ahead a little, but nearly always drifting slowly shoreward, flogging her gear, making a great clatter of blocks. If the soldiers had been half smart they would have seen that she was not under command, and ridden to Dymchurch, taken boat, and come after us. But they had had a severe beating, many of them were wounded, and they had watched our start feeling that we had safely escaped from them. I have never had much opinion of soldiers. Boys generally take their opinions ready made from their elders. I took mine from Marah, who, being a sailor, thought that a soldier was something too silly for words.

As we drifted I went back to Marah to bathe his head with water and to give him drink. He was not conscious; he had even ceased babbling; I was afraid that he could not live for more than a few hours at the most. I had never really liked the man—I had feared him too much to like him—but he had looked after me for so long, and had been, in his rough way, so kind to me, that I cried for him as though he were my only friend. He was the only friend within many miles of me, and now he lay there dying in a boat which was drifting ashore to a land full of enemies.

It was a hateful-looking land, flat and desolate, dank and dirty-looking. The flat, dull, dirty marsh country seemed to be without life; the very grass seemed blighted. And we were drifting ashore to it, fast drifting ashore to the tune of the two drunkards:

> 'There was a ship, and a ship of fame:
> Away, ho! Rise and shine.
> There was a ship, and a ship of fame,
> So rise and shine, my buck o boy.'

A ship manned by such a crew was hardly a ship of fame, I thought. Then it occurred to me that if she went ashore I might escape from her, might even get safely home, or at least get to London (I had no notion how far London might be), where I thought that the Lord Mayor, of whom I had often heard

DRIFTING

as a great man, would send me home. I had
a new half-crown in my pocket; that would
be enough to keep me in food on the road, I
thought. And then, just as I thought that,
a little coast-current spun us in very rapidly,
helped by the wind, for about two hundred
yards. This brought us very close to the
shore, but not quite near enough for me,
who had no great wish to start my journey
wet through.

I gave Marah a last sip of water, left a
bucket of fresh water and a pannikin close to
him, in case he should recover (I never thought
he would), and then began to make up a
little parcel of things to take with me. I was
wearing the clothes of a ship's boy, canvas
trousers, thick blucher shoes, a rough check
shirt, and a straw hat. My own clothes—the
clothes which I had worn when I scrambled
down the fox's earth—were forward, under
the half deck. I went to fetch them, and
got them safely, though the drunkards tried
to stop me, and said that they only wanted
me to sing them a song to be as happy as
kings. However, I got away from them, and
carried my belongings aft. I then took the
tarpaulin boat-rug, which covered our little

Norwegian pram or skiff, on its chocks between the masts. It was rather too large for my purpose, so I cut it in two, using the one half as a bundle-cover. The other half would make a sort of cape or cloak, I thought, and to that end I folded it and slung it over my shoulder. I gave my knife a few turns upon the grindstone, pocketed some twine from one of the lockers, lashed my bundle in its tarpaulin as tightly as I could, and then went aft to the provision lockers to get some stores for the road. I took out a few ship's biscuits, a large hunk of ham, some onions, and the half of a Dutch cheese.

It occurred to me that I ought to eat before I started, as I did not know what might befall upon the road. When I sat down upon the deck to begin my meal, I saw, to my horror, that we were drifting out again. While I had been packing, we had been swept off shore; by this time we were three hundred yards away, still drawing further out to sea. Looking out, I saw that we were drifting into a 'jobble' or tide-race, which seemed to drift obliquely into the shore. This made me feel less frightened, so I turned to my food, ate heartily, and

DRIFTING

took a good swig at the scuttle-butt by way of a morning draught. Then I undid my parcel, packed as much food into it as I possibly could, and lashed it up again in its tarpaulin. I found a few reins and straps in one of the lockers, so I made shoulder-straps of them, and buckled my package to my shoulders. My last preparation was to fill a half-pint glass flask (every man aboard carries one or two of these). Just as I replaced its stopper, we swept into the jobble; the lugger filled on one tack, and lay over, and the spray of a wave came over us. Then we righted suddenly, came up into the wind with our sails slatting, and made a stern-board.

Nearer and nearer came the land; the shore, with its bent grass, seemed almost within catapult shot. I heard the wash of the sea upon the beach, I could see the pebbles on the sands shining as the foam left them. And then, suddenly, the lugger drove ashore upon a bank, stern first. In a moment she had swung round, broadside on to the shoal, heaving over on her side. Every wave which struck her lifted her further in, tossing her over on her starboard side. I could see that the tide was now very nearly fully in, and I knew that the lugger would lie there, high and dry, as soon as it ebbed.

I made Marah as comfortable as I could, and called to the drunkards to come with me. I told them that a revenue cutter was within six miles of us (there was, as it happened, but she was at anchor off Dymchurch), and that they had better be going out of that before they got themselves arrested. For answer they jeered and made catcalls, flinging a marline-spike at me. I tried a second time to make them come ashore, but one of them said, 'Let's do for him,' and the other cheered the proposal with loud yells. Then they came lurching aft at me, so I just slipped over the side, and waded very hurriedly ashore. The water was not deep (it was not up to my thighs in any place), so that I soon reached the sand without wetting my package. Then I looked back to see the two smugglers leaning over the side, watching my movements. One of them was singing—

> 'There was a ship, and a ship of fame:
> Away, ho! Rise and shine'

in a cracked falsetto. The other one was saying, 'You come back, you young cub.'

DRIFTING

But I did not do as they bid. I ran up the beach and as far across the wet grassland as I could without once stopping. When I thought that I was safe, I sat down under some bushes, took off my wet things, and dressed myself in my own clothes. I wrung the water from the wet canvas, repacked my parcel, and seeing a road close to me, turned into it at once, resolved to ask the way to London at the first house. I suppose that it was five o'clock in the morning when I began my journey.

CHAPTER XVII

THE 'BLUE BOAR'

As I stepped out, the adventure, the fight, Marah's wound, all the tumult of the battle, seemed very far away, and as though they had happened to some one else who had told me of them. If my head had not ached so cruelly from the blow which the soldier gave me, I should not have believed that they had really occurred, and that I had seen them and taken part in them. It seemed to me that I was close to my home, that I should soon come to the combe country, where the Gara runs down the valley to the sea, passing the slate quarry, so grey against the copse. The road was good enough, though I was not in good trim for walking after so many days cooped up in the lugger. I stepped forward bravely along a lonely country-side till I saw before me the houses of a town.

I thought that I had better skirt the town, lest I should stumble on the coastguards and rouse their suspicions. It was too early in the morning for a boy to be abroad, and I had no very satisfactory account to give of myself in case anybody questioned me. I knew that if I said that I had been among the smugglers I should be sent to prison. I felt that the magistrate would be too angry to listen to my story, and that they would perhaps send me to prison at once if they ever got hold of me. Magistrates in those days had a great deal of power. They were often illiterate, and they bullied and hectored the people whom they tried. I had seen one or two bad magistrates at home, and I knew how little chance I should stand if I told my unlikely story to a bench in a court-house before such men as they were. So I turned up a small road to the right, avoiding the town, where, as I could see, a good deal of bustle was stirring; indeed, the streets were full of people.

By-and-by, as the sun rose higher, I began to meet people. A few labouring men came past me, one of them carrying a pitchfork. I noticed that they looked at me curiously

One of them spoke, and said, 'You have been in the wars, master!' So I said, 'Yes,' and passed on, wondering what he meant. After I had passed, the man stopped to look back at me. I even heard him take a few steps towards me, before he thought better of it, and went on upon his way. This set me wondering if there were anything strange about my appearance; so, when I came to the little brook or river, which crossed the road a little further on, I went down to a pool where the water was still, and looked at my image in the water. Sure enough, I had an odd appearance. The blow which the soldier gave me had broken the skin of my scalp, not badly, but enough to make an ugly scar. You may be sure that I lost no time in washing my face and head, till no stains showed. I rebuked myself for not having done this while abroad the lugger, when I had splashed my head at the scuttle-butt. I felt all the better for the wash in the brook; but when I took to the road again I had a great fear lest the labourers should hear of the battle, and give out that they had seen a wounded boy going along the road away from the beach.

THE 'BLUE BOAR'

After a mile of lane, I came to a high-road, past a church and houses, all very peaceful and still. I passed these, and wandered on along the high-road, thinking that I had gone many miles from the sea, though, of course, I had only gone a little distance. When one walks a new road, one finds it much longer than it really is. I sat down by the roadside now and then to think of plans. I felt that my best plan would be to go to London, and see the Lord Mayor, who, I felt sure, would help me to get home. But I had not much notion of where London was, and I knew that if I went into a house to ask the road to London, people would suspect that I was running away, and so, perhaps, find out that I had been with the smugglers. I knew that many people there must be smugglers themselves; but then, suppose that I asked at a house where they were friends of the preventives? The smugglers had signs among themselves by which they recognised each other.

They used to scratch the left ear with the left little finger, and then bite the lower lip, before shaking hands with anybody. I thought that I would go into an inn and try these signs on somebody (on the landlord if possible) and then ask his advice. An inn would be a good place, I thought, because the landlord would be sure to buy from the smugglers; besides, in inns there are generally maps of the country, showing the coaching houses, and the days of the fairs. A map of the kind would show me my road, and be a help to me in that way, even if the landlord did not recognise my signs. And yet I was half afraid of trying these signs. I did not want to get back among the smugglers. I only wanted to get to London. I had that foolish belief that the Lord Mayor would help me. I was too young to know better; and besides, I was afraid that my being with the smugglers would, perhaps, get me hanged, if I were caught by one of those magistrates, whom I so much feared.

Presently I came to another little village, rather larger than the last. There was an inn in the main street (the 'Blue Boar'), so I went into the inn-parlour, and looked about me. One or two men were talking earnestly, in low voices, to a sad-faced, weary-looking woman behind the bar. She looked up at me rather sharply as I entered,

THE 'BLUE BOAR' 203

and the men turned round and stared at me made a few more remarks to the woman, and went quickly out. I looked at the woman, scratched my left ear with my left little finger, and bit my lower lip. She caught her breath sharply and turned quite white; evidently she knew that sign extremely well.

'What is it?' she said, 'what's the news? There's been fighting. Where's Dick?'

I said I didn't know where Dick was, but that there had been fighting, sure enough; and the preventives had been beaten off.

'Ah,' she said, 'and the stuff? Did they get the stuff off?'

I said, I believed that it had got off safely.

'I believe everybody's bewitched to-day,' she said, bursting into tears. 'Oh, Dick, come back to me. Come back to me. Oh, why did I ever marry a man like you?'

She cried bitterly for a few minutes. Then she asked me a lot of questions about the fight. One question she repeated many times: 'Was there a grey horse in the second string?'

But this I could not answer certainly. All the time that we were talking, she was crying and laughing by turns. Whenever a person entered (even if it were only the milkman) she turned white and shook, as though expecting the police.

'It's the palpitation,' she would explain. 'That and the sizzums.'

Then she would go on laughing and crying by turns until some one else came in.

Presently the landlady looked at me rather hard. 'Here,' she said, 'you are not one of them. You've run away from home, you have. What are you doing here?'

I said that I was on my way to London.

'To London,' she said. 'What's a boy like you going to London for? How are you going?'

I said that I was going to walk there, to see the Lord Mayor.

'To—see—the—Lord Mayor,' she repeated. 'Is the boy daft, or what?'

I blushed, and hung my head, for I did not like to be laughed at.

'What are you going to see the Lord Mayor for?' she asked with a smile.

I answered that he would send me home to my friends, as he was always generous to people in distress. She laughed very heartily

THE 'BLUE BOAR'

when I had said this: but still, not unkindly. Then she asked me a lot of questions about my joining the smugglers, about my friends at home (particularly if they were well off), and about the money I had to carry me to London. When I had told her everything, she said,—

'Well, why don't you write to your friends from here? Surely that's a more sensible plan than going to London—why, London's seventy miles. Write to your friends from here. They will get the letter in three or four days. They will be here within a week from now. That's a wiser thing to do than going to London. Why, you'd die in a ditch before you got half-way.'

'I shouldn't,' I answered hotly

'Well, if you didn't you'd get taken up. It's all the same,' she answered. 'You stop here and write to your friends. I will see that the letter goes all right. I suppose,' she continued, 'I suppose your friends wouldn't let me be a loser by you? They'd pay for what you ate and that?'

'Yes,' I said, 'of course they will.'

'What's your name?' she said sharply.

I told her

'Oh,' she said. 'Jim—Jim Davis. Let's

see that shirt of yours, to see if it's got your name on. I been taken in once or twice before. One has to look alive, keeping an inn.'

Luckily my name was upon my shirt and stockings, so that she accepted my story without further talk, especially as the contents of my package showed her that I had told her the truth about the lugger.

'I don't know what Dick will say,' she said. 'But now you come up, and I'll dress your head. You'll have to lie low, remember. It won't do for a smuggler like you to be seen about here. So till your friends come, you'll keep pretty dark, remember.'

She led me upstairs to plaster my wound. Then she put me into a little bedroom on one of the upper floors, and told me to stay there till she called me. There were one or two books upon the shelf, including a funny one with woodcuts, a collection of tales and ballads, such as the pedlars used to sell in those days. With this book, and with a piece of paper and a pencil, I passed the morning more happily than I can say.

My head felt quite easy after it had been dressed and bandaged. My troubles were nearly over, I thought. In a week my friends would be there to fetch me away. In three days they would get my letter and hear all about my adventures; so as I wrote I almost sang aloud; I was so happy at the thought of my sorrows being ended. Mrs Dick (I never learned her real name till some years afterwards) brought me some bread and cheese at mid-day. As I ate, she sealed and addressed my letter for me, and took it over to the post-house, so that the postman could carry it to meet the mail, as it drove past from Rye towards London.

After my mid-day meal I felt strangely weary; perhaps all my excitements had been too much for me. When Mrs Dick came back to say that she had posted my letter I was almost asleep; but her manner was so strange that it roused me. She could hardly speak from anxiety and terror.

'Oh,' she cried, 'they have raised the whole country. My Dick'll be taken. He will. He will. They're riding all through the land arresting everybody. And they're going to hang them all, they say, as soon as they can give them their trials.'

She cried and cried as though her heart

would break. I did what I could to comfort her, but still she cried hysterically, and for all that afternoon she sobbed and laughed in the little upper bedroom, only going out at rare intervals, to peep into the bar, where her servant served the guests.

Towards five o'clock, the servant came running upstairs to say that a lot of the smugglers had been taken. 'A whole boat-load,' the girl said, so that now it would 'all come out, and master would be hanged.' Mrs Dick told her not to talk in that way of her master, but to find out if any of the men had peached.

When the girl had gone she seemed to collect herself. She became a different woman in a minute.

'Well, if he's taken,' she said, 'they'll be here. That's very sure. They'll search the premises. They mustn't find you here, Mr Jim. If they find you, they'll question you, and you know too much by a long way.'

'Shall I go?' I asked. 'I'm willing to clear out, if you wish.'

'Go?' she said. 'Go? I will turn no poor boy out into the road. I have a boy of my own, somewhere walking the world. No,

THE 'BLUE BOAR'

I'll put you in the drawing-room. Come with me, and don't make a noise.'

She led me downstairs to the foot of the lowest staircase, which was rather broad, with high steps of stout old oak.

'Look,' she said, as she stepped away from me—I suppose to touch some secret spring—'this is the drawing-room.'

As she spoke, the two lowest stairs suddenly rolled back upon a sort of hinge, showing a little room, not much bigger than a couple of barrels, arranged underneath them. There were blankets and a mattress upon the floor of this little room, besides several packages like those which I had seen in the lugger.

'You'll have to stay here, Jim,' she said kindly. 'But first of all I must get together Dick's papers and that. Come on and help me.'

Very soon she had gathered together a few papers and packets of tobacco and lace, which might have brought Dick into trouble. She laid these away in the recesses of the secret room, and told me to get inside, and go to sleep, and above all things to keep very still if people came along upon the stairs. I crept inside, rather frightened, and lay down among the blankets, to get some rest. Then Mrs Dick swung the two stairs back into their place, a spring clicked, and I was a prisoner in the dark, shut up in the drawing-room.

CHAPTER XVIII

TRACKED

It was very dark in the drawing-room under the stairs, and rather stuffy, for the only light and air admitted came through a little narrow crack, about six inches long, and half an inch across at its broadest. There was a strong smell of mice, among other smells; and the mice came scampering all over me before I had lain there long. I lay as still as I could, because of what Mrs Dick had said, and by-and-by I fell asleep in spite of the mice, and slept until it was dark.

I was awakened by the rolling back of the stairs. As I started up, thinking that I was captured, I saw Mrs Dick standing over me with a candle in her hand.

'Hush Jim,' she said. 'Get out quickly. Don't ask any questions. Get out at once. You can't stay here any longer.'

'What has happened?' I asked. 'Where

is your husband? Has your husband come home?'

'Yes,' she said. 'And you must go. They're coming after you. You were seen in the lugger with an axe in your hands. A man who passed you on the road after, saw you in the lugger. He was with the soldiers, and now he's given an information. Mary, the girl, heard it down at the magistrate's, where the inquest is. And so you must go. Besides, I want the drawing-room for my Dick. He has come back, and they'll be after him quite likely. He was seen, they say. So he must lie low till we've arranged the alibi, as they call it. Everybody has to have an alibi. And so my Dick'll have one, just to make sure. Mind your head against the stair.'

I crawled out, rubbing my eyes.

'Where shall I go to?' I asked.

'Oh,' she said. 'Until we find out, you had better go in the stable, in among the feed in the box, or covered up in the hay.'

When she had settled her husband safely into the drawing-room, she bustled me out of doors into the stable, which stood in the yard at the back of the inn. She put me into a mass of loose hay, in one of the unused stalls.

'There,' she said. 'They'll never look for you there. Don't get hay-fever and begin to sneeze, though. Here's your parcel for you. It wouldn't do to leave that about in the house, would it?'

She wished me good night and bustled back to the inn, to laugh and jest as though nothing was happening, and as though she had no trouble in the world.

I lay very quietly in my warm nest in the hay, feeling lonely in that still stable after my nights in the lugger among the men. The old horse stamped once or twice, and the stable cat came purring to me, seeking to be petted. The church clock struck nine, and rang out a chime. Shortly after nine I heard the clatter of many horses' hooves coming along the road, and then the noise of cavalry jingling and clattering into the inn yard. A horse whinnied, the old horse in the stable whinnied in answer. A curt voice called to the men to dismount, and for some one to hold the horses. I strained my ears to hear any further words, but some one banging on a door (I guessed it to be the inn door) drowned the orders.

Then some one cried out, 'Well, break it in then. Don't come asking me.'

After that there was more banging, an excited cry from a woman, and a few minutes of quiet.

I crept from my hiding-place to the window, so that I might see what was happening. The whole yard was full of cavalry. A couple of troopers were holding horses quite close to the door. By listening carefully, I could hear what they were saying.

'Yes,' said one of them; 'I got a proper lick myself. I shan't mind if they do get caught. They say there's some of them caught in a boat.'

'Yes,' said his mate; 'three. And they do say we shall find a boy here as well as the other fellow. There was a boy aboard all night. And he's been tracked here. He's as good as caught, I reckon.'

'I suppose they'll all be hanged?' said the first.

'Yes,' said the other. 'Won't be no defence for them. Neck or nothing. Hey?'

Then they passed out of earshot, leading

their horses. I was so horribly scared that I was almost beside myself. What could I do? Where could I go? Where could I hide? The only door and window opened on to the courtyard. The loft was my only chance. I snatched up my parcel, and ran to the little ladder (nailed to the wall) which led to the loft, and climbed up as though the hounds were after me.

Even in the loft I was not much better off. There was a heap of hay and a few bundles of straw lying at one end, and two great swing-doors, opening on to the courtyard, through which the hay and straw had been passed to shelter. It was plainly useless to lie down in the straw. That would be the first place searched. I should be caught at once if I hid among the straw. Then it occurred to me that the loft must lead to a pigeon-house. I had seen a pigeon-house above and at one end of the stable, and I judged that the loft would communicate with it. It was not very light, but, by groping along the end wall, I came to a little latched door leading to another little room. This was the pigeon-house, and as I burst into it, closing the door behind me, the many pigeons rustled and stirred upon their nests and perches.

It was darker in the pigeon-house than in the loft, but I could see that the place was bigger than the loft itself, and this gave me hope that there would be an opening at the back of it away from the yard. I had not much time, I knew, because the troopers were already trying to open the stable-door below me. I could hear them pounding and grumbling. Just as I heard them say, 'That's it. The bar lifts up. There you are'—showing that they had found how to open the door—I came to a little door at the back, a little rotten door, locked and bolted with rusty cobwebbed iron. Very cautiously I turned the lock and drew the bolts back. The latch creaked under my thumb for the first time in many years. I was outside the door on a little, rotten, wooden landing, from which a flight of wooden steps led downward. I saw beyond me a few farm-buildings, a byre, several pigsties, and three disused waggons. Voices sounded in the stable as I climbed down the steps. I heard a man say, 'He might be in the loft. We might look there.' And then I touched the ground, and scurried quickly past the shelters to the outer wall.

Happily for me, the wall was well-grown with ivy, so that I could climb to the top. There was a six-foot drop on the far side into a lane; but it was now neck or nothing, so I let myself go. I came down with a crack which made my teeth rattle, my parcel spun away into a bed of nettles, and I got well stung in fishing it out. Then I strapped it on my back and turned along the lane in the direction which (as I judged) led me away from the sea. As I stepped out on my adventures, I heard the ordered trample of horses leaving the inn-yard together to seek elsewhere. The lane soon ended at a stile, which led into a field. I saw a barn or shed just beyond the stile, and in the shed there was a heap of hay, which smelt a little mouldy. I lay down upon it, determined to wake early, and creep back to the inn before anybody stirred in the village.

'Ah, well,' I said to myself before I fell asleep, 'in a week's time they will be here to take me home. Then my troubles will be over.'

I remember that all my fear of the troops

was gone. I felt so sure that all would be well in the morning. So, putting my parcel under my head as a pillow, I snuggled down into the hay, and very soon fell asleep.

I was awakened in the morning by the entrance of an old cart-horse, who came to smell at the hay. It was light enough to see where I was going, so I opened my knapsack and made a rough breakfast before setting out. Overnight I had planned to go back to the inn. In the cool of the morning that plan did not seem so very wise as I had thought it. I was almost afraid to put it into practice. However, I went back along the lane. With some trouble, I got over the tall brick wall down which I had dropped the night before. Then I climbed up to the pigeon-house, down the loft-ladder, into the inn-yard, to the broken back door of the tavern. The door hung from one hinge, with its lower panels kicked in just as the soldiers had left it. The inn was open to anybody who cared to enter.

I entered cautiously, half expecting to find a few soldiers billeted there. But the place was empty. I went from room to room, finding no one; Mrs Dick seemed to have disappeared. One of the rooms was in disorder. A few broken glasses were on the floor; a chair lay on its side under the table. I went upstairs. I tapped at the outside of the drawing-room. No answer there; all was still there. I listened attentively for some sound of breathing; none came. No one was inside. I went all over the house. No one was there. I was alone in the 'Blue Boar,' the only person in the house. I could only guess that Mr and Mrs Dick had been arrested. To be sure they might have run away together during the night. I did not quite know what to think.

In my wanderings, I came to the bar, which I found in great disorder; the bench was upset, jugs and glasses were scattered on the floor, and the blinds had not been pulled up. Although I had some fear of being seen from outside, I pulled up the blinds to let in a little light, so that I might look at the coaching-map which hung at one end of the bar. When I passed behind the bar to trace out for myself the road to London, I saw an open book lying on a shelf among the bottles. It was a copy of Captain Johnson's *Lives of the Highwaymen and Pirates*, lying open at the life of Captain Roberts, the famous pirate of Whydah. Someone must have been reading it when the soldiers entered.

I looked at it curiously, for it was open at the portrait of Roberts. Underneath the portrait were a few words written in pencil in a clumsy scrawl. I read them over, expecting some of the ordinary schoolboy nonsense.

'Captain Roberts was a bad one. *Jim.* Don't come back here. The lobsters is around.' That was all the message. But I saw at once that it was meant for me; that Mrs Dick, knowing that I should come back, had done her best to leave a warning for me. 'Lobsters,' I knew, was the smugglers' slang for soldiers; and if the lobsters were dangerous to me it was plain that I was wanted for my innocent share in the fight. I looked through the book for any further message; but there was no other entry, except a brief pencilled memorandum of what some one had paid for groceries many years before, at some market town not named.

CHAPTER XIX

THE ROAD TO LONDON

You may be sure that I lost no time in leaving the inn. I merely noted the way to London from the coaching-map and hurried out, repeating the direction so that I should not forget. It was a bright, cool morning: and I walked very briskly for a couple of hours, when I sat down to rest by the roadside, under a patch of willows, which grew about a little bubbling brook. Presently I saw that a little way ahead of me were three gipsy-looking people (a boy with his father and mother) sitting by the road resting. They got up, after I had been there for twenty minutes or so, and came along the road towards me, bowed under their bundles. I got up, too, intending to continue my journey; but when I was about to pass them, the man drew up in front of me.

'Beg your pardon, young master,' he said; 'but could you tell me the way to Big Ben?'

'But that's in London,' I said. 'That's in London, at the House of Parliament.'

'What!' he cried. 'You don't mean to tell me that us have come the wrong road?'

'Yes,' I said. 'You're going the wrong way for London.'

'Then take that,' cried the man, giving me a shove, just as the woman flung her shawl over my head. I stepped back, for the shove was no light one; but just behind me the boy had crouched on all fours (he had evidently practised the trick) so that I went headlong over him, and had a nasty fall into the road.

'Stop his mouth, Martha,' said the man: and stop it she did, with her ragged old shawl, in which she had evidently carried the provisions of the gang.

'What's he got on him?' said the woman, as the man rummaged through my pockets.

'Only a prince and a chive,' said the man, disgustedly, meaning my half-crown and a jack-knife.

'Well,' said the woman, 'his jacket's better than Bill's, and we'll have his little port-manteau, what's more.'

In another minute they had my suit

stripped from me; and I had the sight of dirty little Bill, the tramper's boy, putting on my things.

'Here,' said the woman. 'You put on Bill's things. They're good enough for you. And don't you dare breathe a word of what we done.'

'Yes,' said the man, as Bill buttoned up his jacket, and took my little bundle in his hand. 'You keep your little jaw shut or *I*'ll come after you.'

'Oh, Mother,' said Bill. 'Don't I look a young swell, neither?'

For answer, his mother grabbed him by the arm, and the three hurried away from me in the direction from which I had come. The man looked back and made a face at me, shaking his fist. I was left penniless in the road. A milestone told me that I was sixty-six miles from London.

I was now at the end of my resources; almost too miserable to cry. I did not know what was to become of me. I could only wander along the road, in a dazed sort of way, wishing for Marah. I was wretched and faint, and Marah was so strong and careless. Then I said to myself that Marah was dead, and that I should soon be dead, for I had neither food nor money. The smugglers had talked of shipwrecks once or twice. I had heard them say that a man could live for three days without food or drink, in fair weather; and that without food, drinking plenty of water, he could live for three weeks. They were very wild talkers, to be sure; but I remembered this now and got comfort from it. Surely, I thought, I shall be able to last for a week, and in a week I ought to be near London. Besides, I can eat grass; and perhaps I shall find a turnip, or a potato, or a partridge's nest with young ones still in it; and perhaps I shall be able to earn a few coppers by opening gates, or holding horses.

I plucked up wonderfully when I thought of all these things; though I did not at all like wearing Bill's clothes. I felt that I looked like a dirty young tramp, and that anybody who saw me would think that I was one. Besides, I had always hated dirt and untidiness, and the feeling that I carried both about me was hateful.

But Bill's clothes were to be a great help to me before noon that day. As I wandered along the road, wondering where I could get something to eat (for I was now very hungry), I came to a turnpike. The turnpike-keeper was cleaning his windows, outside his little house. When he saw me, he just popped his head inside the door, and said something to some people inside. His manner frightened me; but I was still more frightened when two Bow Street runners (as we called detectives then) and a yeomanry officer came out of the house, and laid hold of me.

'That's your boy, sir,' said the turnpike-keeper.

'Come on in here,' said the officer, 'and give an account of yourself.'

They led me into the room, where they were eating some bread and cheese.

'He doesn't answer the description,' said one of the men, glancing at a paper.

'I'm not so sure about that,' said the officer. 'He's the exact height, and that's the same coloured hair.'

'Now I come to think of it,' said the keeper, 'I believe I saw that boy pass along here this morning, along of two trampers. That coat with the pocket torn. Yes, and red lining showing. I thought I'd seen them.'

'Well, boy,' said the officer 'what's your name?'

'Jim Davis,' I answered.

'What were you doing with the two trampers, Jim?' he asked.

'Please, sir,' I said, 'I wasn't doing anything with them.'

'Ah,' said one of the runners. 'These young rogues is that artful, they never do nothing anywhere.'

'You'll live to be hanged, I know,' said the other runner.

'What were you doing with the smugglers?' asked the officer suddenly, staring hard at my face, to watch for any change of expression.

But I was ready for him. A boy is often better able to keep his countenance than a grown man. With masters and aunts, and game-keepers all down upon him, he lives a hunted life. He gets lots of practice in keeping his countenance. A grown man often gets very little.

'What smugglers, sir?' I asked as boldly as I could.

THE ROAD TO LONDON

'The men you sailed with from Etaples,' said the officer.

'Sailed with?' I asked, feeling that I was done for.

'Didn't the horses splash about, when you cut the cable?' said the officer, with a smile.

This time I thought I had better not answer. I looked as puzzled as I could, and looked from one face to the other, as though for enlightenment.

'Now, Jim,' said one of the runners. 'It's no good. Tell us all about the smugglers, and we'll let you go.'

'We know you're the boy we want,' said the captain. 'Make a clean breast of it, and perhaps you will get off with transportation.'

'Now don't look so innocent,' said the other runner. 'Tell us what we want to know, or we'll make you.'

Now somewhere I had read that the police bullied suspected persons in this way. If you make a guilty person believe that you know him to be guilty, you can also get him to confess if you startle him sufficiently. It occurred to me that this was what these men were doing, especially as they had not been sure of me when I came into the room.

I had some twenty or thirty seconds in which to think of an answer, for the three men spoke one after the other, without giving me a chance to speak. I shook my head, putting on a puzzled look.

'I beg your pardon, sir,' I said, speaking rather roughly, in the accent which Bill had used. 'I think there's some mistake.'

'Oh, I think not,' said the officer. 'Suppose I tell you how many men were in the lugger?'

But here we were stopped by the arrival of a chaise outside. A man entered hurriedly.

'It's all right, Gray,' the new-comer called to the officer. 'We have the boy. We caught him back there, along the road, with a couple of gipsies. There can be no doubt about it. The clothes and bundle are just as they're described in the advertisement. Who have you here?'

'Oh, a boy we brought in on suspicion,' said the officer. 'Shall we let him go?'

'Well, who is he?' asked the new arrival. 'Eh, boy? Who are you?'

'A poor boy,' I answered.

'How do you make a living?' he asked. 'Little boys, like you, oughtn't to be about on the roads you know. What d'ye do for a living?'

I am afraid it was rather a bold statement; but I cried out that I could sing ballads.

'Oh, Jim. So you sing ballads, do you?' said the officer. 'Get on to that chair and sing us a ballad.'

But I was cunning and wary. 'Please, sir,' I said, 'I'm very hungry. I don't sing, except for my dinner and a sixpence.'

'So you defy the law already, do you?' said the new-comer. 'Well. Eat some bread and cheese. and I will give you sixpence for a song.'

So I sat down very thankfully, and made a good dinner at the table. I pretended to pay no attention to the officers; but really I listened very eagerly to all that they said. I gathered that the new-comer was a coast-guard naval captain, of the name of Byrne, and I felt that he half-suspected and half-liked me, without thinking very much about me one way or the other. When I had finished my dinner—and I ate enough to last me till the night—I got upon my chair, without being pressed, and sang the ballad of 'The White Cockade,' then very popular all over the West country. My voice was not bad in those days, and I was used to singing; indeed, people sang more then than they do now. Everybody sang.

Captain Byrne seemed puzzled by my voice, and by my cultivated accent. 'Who taught you to sing?' he asked.

So I answered that I had been in the village choir at home; which was true enough

'And where was that?' he asked.

For a moment I thought that I would trust him, and tell him everything. Then, very foolishly, I determined to say nothing, so I said that it was a long way away, and that I had come from thence after my father had died. He whispered something to Mr Gray, the other officer; and they looked at me curiously. They both gave me a sixpenny piece for my ballad; and then they went out. Captain Byrne stopped at the door. 'Look here,' he said, 'You take my advice and go home. You will come to no good, leading this wandering life.'

When they had gone, I went out also, and watched their chaise disappear. The last that I saw of them was the two top-hats of the runners, sticking up at the back of the conveyance, like little black chimneys.

I felt very glad that Bill was taken up, evidently in mistake for me. It seemed a fitting reward. But at the same time I knew that the mistake might be found out at any moment; and that I should be searched for as soon as Bill had cleared himself. I walked slowly away from the turnpike, so that the keeper might not suspect me, and then I nipped over a stile, and ran away across country, going inland, away from the sea, as fast as I could travel. I could tell my direction by the sun, and I kept a westerly course, almost due west, for three or four hours, till I was tired out.

It was a lonely walk, too; hardly anything but wild, rather marshy country, with few houses, few churches, and no bigger town than the tiniest of villages. At about six o'clock that afternoon, when I had gone some sixteen miles since daybreak, I felt that I could go no further, and began to cast about for a lodging-place.

CHAPTER XX

THE GIPSY CAMP

I plodded on till I came to a sort of copse or little wood, where I expected to find shelter. Supper I had resolved to do without; I wished to keep my shilling for dinner and breakfast the next day. As I came up to the copse hedge I saw that some gipsies were camped there. They had a fine travelling waggon drawn up on some waste ground near at hand; they had also pitched three or four beehive huts, made of bent poles, covered with sacks. They were horse-dealers and basket-makers, as one could see from the drove of lean horses and heap of wicker-work near the waggon. Several children were playing about among the huts. Some women were at their basket-making by the waggon. A middle-aged man, smoking a pipe, stood by the hedge, mending what looked like an enormous butterfly net. In spite of my adventure on the road, I was

THE GIPSY CAMP

not at all frightened by these gipsies, because I liked their looks, and I knew now that I had only my shilling to lose, and that I could earn a dinner at any time by singing a ballad.

The middle-aged man looked rather hard at me as I came near, and called out in a strange language to his people in the tents. They came about me at the call, and stared at me very strangely, as though I was a queer beast escaped from a menagerie. Then, to my great surprise, the man pointed to my forehead, and all the gipsies stared at my forehead, repeating those queer words which Marah had used so long before in the gorse-clump—'Orel. Orel. Adartha Cay.' They seemed very pleased and proud; they clapped their hands and danced, as though I was a little prince. All the time they kept singing and talking in their curious language. Now and then one of them would come up to me and push back my cap to look at my hair, which was of a dark brown colour, with a dash of reddy gold above my forehead.

I learned afterwards that gipsies held sacred all boys with hair like mine. They call the ruddy tinge over the forehead 'the cross upon crutches'; for long ago, they say, a great gipsy hero had that mark upon his brow in lines of fire; and to this day all people with a fiery lock of hair, they believe, bring luck to them.

When the gipsies had danced for some twenty minutes, the elderly man (who seemed to be a chief among them) begged me (in English) with many profound bows and smiles, to enter their waggon. I had heard that the gipsies stole little children; but as I had never heard of them stealing a boy of my age I did not fear them. So I entered the waggon as he bade me, and very neat and trim it was. Here a man produced a curious red suit of clothes, rather too small for me; but still a lot better than Bill's rags. He begged me to put it on, which I did. I know now that it was the red magical suit in which the gipsies dress their magical puppets on St. John's Eve; but as I did not then know this, I put it on quite willingly, wishing that it fitted better.

Then we came out again among the huts, and all the other gipsies crowded round me, laughing and clapping their hands; for now, they thought, their tribe would have wonderful luck wherever they went. The women put a pot upon the fire, ready for supper. Everybody treated me (very much to my annoyance) as though I were a fairy child. When-

THE GIPSY CAMP

ever I spoke, they bowed and laughed and clapped their hands, crying out in their wild language, till I could have boxed their ears.

When supper was ready, they brought me to the place of honour by the fire, and fed me with all the delicacies of the gipsy race. We had hedgehog baked in a clay cover—though I did not much like him—and then a stew of poultry and pheasant (both stolen, I'm afraid) with bread baked in the ashes; and wonderful tea, which they said cost eighteen shillings a pound. They annoyed me very much by the way in which they bowed and smirked, but they really meant to be kind, and I had sense enough to know that while I was with them I should be practically safe from the runners and yeomanry. After supper they made me up a bed in the waggon. The next morning before daybreak we started off, horses, waggon, and all, away towards the west; going to Portsmouth Fair, the man said, to sell their horses.

I had not been very long among the gipsies when I discovered that I was as much a prisoner as a pet. They would never let me out of their sight. If I tried to get away by myself, one of the children, or a young woman would follow me, or rather, come in the same direction, and pretend not to be following me; but all the time noting where I went, and heading me off carefully if I went too far from the caravan. Before the end of the first day I was wondering how it would all finish, and whether they meant to make a gipsy of me. They were very careful not to let me be seen by other travellers. When the road was clear, they would let me follow the caravan on foot; but when people drove past us, and whenever we came to a village (they always avoided the big towns) they hurried me into the waggon, and kept me from peeping out. At night, when we pitched our camp, after a long day's journey of sixteen or seventeen hours, they gave me a bed inside the caravan; and the elderly chief laid his blankets on the waggon floor, between my bed and the door, so that I should not get out. I lived with the gipsies in this way for three whole days.

I did not like it any better as time went on. I kept thinking of how I should escape, and worrying about the anxiety at home, now that my letter must have reached them. I did not think any more about the police. I felt that they would give me no more trouble; but my

THE GIPSY CAMP 237

distress at not being able to get away from these gipsies was almost more than I could bear. On the afternoon of the third day I made a dash for freedom, but the chief soon caught me and brought me back, evidently very much displeased, and muttering something about stealing the red coat.

About mid-day on the fourth day, as we were passing through a village, it chanced that a drove of sheep blocked up the road. The caravan stopped and I managed to get down from the waggon, with my gaoler, to see what was happening in the road. The sheep were very wild, and the drover was a boy who did not know how to drive them. The way was blocked for a good ten minutes, so that I had time to look about me. While we waited, a donkey-cart drove up, with two people inside it, dressed in the clothes of naval sailors—white trousers, blue, short, natty jackets (with red and green ribbons in the seams), and with huge clubbed pigtails under their black, glazed hats. One of them was evidently ill, for he lay back against the back-board and did not speak. I noticed also that he had not been to sea for a long time, as his beard was long and unkempt. The other, who drove the cart, was a one-legged man, very short and broad, with a thick black stubble on his cheeks. He was a hearty person with a voice like a lion's roar. They had rigged up Union Jacks on the donkey's blinkers, they had a pilot jack upon the shaft, and a white ensign on a flag-pole tied to the back-board. The body of the cart was all sprigged out with streamers of ribbon as thick as horses' tails, and there were placards fixed to the sides of the donkey's collar. They were clumsily scrawled as follows:—

> Pity the Braiv English Seamen,
> Wonded in the Wars,
> Help them as cannot help theirselves,
> We have Bled for our nativland.
> Nelson and Bronte.

This wonderful conveyance pulled up among the sheep. The one-legged man stood upright in the cart, called for three cheers, and at once began to roar out the never-ending ballad of the battle of Belle Isle:—

> At the battle of Belle Isle,
> I was there all the while, etc., etc.

Everybody clustered round to listen, and to admire the turn-out.

I could not get very near to the cart, because of the press; but I noticed quite suddenly that

THE GIPSY CAMP 239

the sick man was staring rather hard at me from under the rim of his glazed hat, which was jammed down over his eyes. The eyes seemed familiar. There was something familiar in the figure, covered up, as it was, with the rough beard, and with a ship's boat-cloak. It reminded me of Marah, somehow, and yet it could not possibly be Marah; and yet the man was staring hard at me.

A countryman came out of an inn with a mug of drink for the singer, who checked his song at about the hundred-and-fiftieth stanza, to take the mug with a 'Thank ye, mate,' and hand it to his sick friend. The sick man took the mug with his left hand, opening the fingers curiously, and still looking hard at me. My heart gave a great jump, for there were three blue rings tattooed on one of the fingers. The man waved his mug towards me. 'Hoo, hoo, hoo,' he cried, imitating an owl with his weak voice. 'Hoo, hoo, hoo.' Then he clapped his right hand across his mouth to warn me to be silent, and drank, with a bow to the giver.

It *was* Marah, after all. At this moment the caravan started, and the man urged me to enter the waggon again. I did so; but as I turned away, Marah smiled in an absurd manner at me, and bowed three times, making everybody laugh. That made me feel sure that he would help me to escape, and to get home again. I could not help laughing at his trick of dressing up as 'a braiv English seaman, wonded in the war.' Had the people known in what wars he had been wounded, they would not have been so free with their kindness, perhaps.

It occurred to me that Marah had made the owl's cry (or night signal) to show me that I might expect him at night. So when the gipsies went to bed that night I lay awake among them, pretending to be fast asleep. It was very dark, shut up in the waggon. The gipsies slept heavily, and I could hear the horses outside, cropping on the grass and snorting. Once or twice I heard a clock strike very far away. Then I fell asleep, I think, in spite of my excitement. I woke with a start, because just outside the waggon came the wild crying of an owl: and then, at that instant, a banging of guns and pistols. A voice cried out: 'The horses. Save the horses.' Some one screamed 'Help! help!' in a falsetto. More guns banged and cracked, and I heard a rush of hoofs as

THE GIPSY CAMP 241

the drove of horses stampeded. The gipsies in the waggon rushed out as one man to save the precious horses. I rushed out after them, and there was Marah with his one-legged friend, crouched under the waggon, waiting for me.

'Well, Jim,' he said; 'nip this way, quick. We have a suit of clothes all ready for you.'

So they hurried me away to their little cart, where I found a boy's suit, which I was glad to put on, as of course I never wore the precious red suit in bed.

'Those were good fire-crackers,' said Marah's friend. 'They made the horses run.'

'Yes,' said Marah. 'I knew we could clear the gipsies out of the way and get Jim clear. Well, Jim, my son, I'm not strong enough to talk much. I reckon I have done with night-riding since I got this slug in my chest. But here we are again, bound home, my son, with not much shot in the locker.'

'You be quiet,' said his friend; 'you'll be getting your wound bad. Get up, Neddy.'

We trotted off to a little inn which stood at some distance from the gipsies' camp.

The next morning, after a comfortable night in bed, I asked Marah how he had escaped. He told me that when the lugger drove ashore, one or two smugglers who had hidden in the dunes, crept down to her and carried him ashore. The two others, the drunkards, were too noisy to bring off. They were captured, and condemned to serve in the Navy. Marah's wound was not very severe; but he had had a great shock, and would not be able to exert himself for many weeks. An old smuggler (the one-legged man) had dressed his wound for him, and had then disguised him as I saw him, with a beard and naval clothes. One of the many Captains Sharp had advanced money for the journey home; but to avoid suspicion they had rigged up their donkey-cart, and worked their way as poor sea-ballad singers.

'And now,' said Marah, 'I heard tell in Kent that you'd written home by the mail-coach, a full five days ago. Well, Jim, we're near the coach-road here. I reckon you're friends'll be coming to see you by to-day's coach. If we go out into the road, to the "Bold Sawyer" yonder, where they change horses and wait, I reckon you'll be able to save them some of their journey. Hey, Sally,' he cried to the waitress, 'what time does the Plymouth mail pass by?"

THE GIPSY CAMP 243

'At eleven o'clock,' said Sally.

'At six bells, Jim,' said Marah, 'you'll see your folk again. On that I'll wager my best new silver buttons.'

The clock struck ten.

It was a fair sunny summer's day, with a brisk wind blowing, when we ranged ourselves across the road outside the 'Bold Sawyer.' The coach-horn, sounding in the distance, was drawing rapidly nearer; we could hear the rhythm of the sixteen hoofs. Presently the horses swung round the corner; we saw the coachman flick his leaders so that he might dash up to the inn in style. Then as they galloped up I saw two well-known figures sitting outside, well muffled up. They were Hugh and Mrs Cottier. We had flags in our hands, so we waved them and shouted. The one-legged man roared out his doings at the battle of Belle Isle. I heard Hugh shouting at the top of his voice, 'Look, Mother. It's Jim. It's Jim.' We had a great dinner at the 'Bold Sawyer' at one o'clock that day. We had hardly finished at half-past three, when the mail-coach stopped for us, to take us on our first stage home.

I need only add a few words. Hugh became a 'parson fellow,' as Marah had put it; while I, in time, went to Jamaica as a planter. Marah and the one-legged man took the Gara Mill together, and did very well at it. Mr Cottier is now a Captain in the Portugese Navy. Mrs Cottier keeps house for me here on the Gara. We are all a good deal older; but we keep well. Marah and I are planning a new adventure; for old Van Horn's treasure is still among the coral, and some day we are going to try for it.

THE END